Praying

is

Not

for

Wimps

© 2004 Freddy Davis

ISBN 1-58961-273-6

PageFree Publishing, Inc.
109 South Farmer Street
Otsego, MI 49078

Unless otherwise stated, all Scripture references are taken from the Holy Bible, NEW INTERNATIONAL VERSION®. Copyright © 1973, 1978, 1984 International Bible Society. All rights reserved throughout the world. Used by permission of International Bible Society.

NEW INTERNATIONAL VERSION® and NIV® are registered trademarks of International Bible Society. Use of either trademark for the offering of goods or services requires the prior written consent of International Bible Society.

Praying Is Not For Wimps

By
Freddy Davis

Table of Contents

Introduction i

Chapter 1 - Moving Beyond Prayer Games 1

Chapter 2 - Understanding the Unique Qualities of God 9

Chapter 3 - Why We Can Connect With God 23

Chapter 4 - Praying is More Than a Formula 31

Chapter 5 - How to Get Close to God 49

Chapter 6 - The Place Where the Body Touches the Spirit .. 65

Chapter 7 - Developing the Discipline to Pray 83

Notes 97

Dedication

To my mom
whose prayers for me over the years
have been the foundation stone for my life.

Acknowledgments

My special thanks to:
Jenny Farah,
R.E. Ashmore, DDS
and
Barbara Slaughter
whose kind support made this book a reality.

Additional thanks go to:
My wife, Deborah,
Sondra Turner, PhD
and
T.W. Hunt, PhD
who challenged me to take this book to a higher level.

Introduction

I had just finished reading a great book on prayer and it was powerful. It caused me to have this overwhelming sense that I wanted to be in the presence of God. I made up my mind, right then, that this time I was going to begin having a "quiet time" and I would not let it slide. I began getting up early every morning, and the fire in my belly burned strong. But after a couple of weeks, a morning came along when I was extra tired. When the alarm clock went off, I rolled over and hit the *snooze* button. I figured another ten minutes would be OK. But when it went off again, I was still tired. I thought, "OK, if I miss one day it will be all right." So I missed that morning. Then for the next couple of days I was able to get up, but somehow it wasn't as exciting as it had been before. Then I missed another day, and another. By the end of the third week, I was back to my old ways of not having a quiet time, and was beating myself up because I didn't have the willpower to be consistent. I had been at this place before. I always hated that I was not a powerful prayer warrior, but what is a person to do?

Over the years, as a Christian, I have tried to put a priority on prayer. In an effort to become more knowledgeable and effective in my prayer life, I have tried to learn from my own personal experiences and from both formal and informal study and research. It is always good to learn more in order to have an intellectual understanding of the prayer process. But my purpose in doing all of this study was not simply to have a better grasp of the subject of prayer. Rather, it was to actually become more effective in my praying. I wanted this for myself and I wanted to have the ability to teach other people to do the same. But in spite of all of my study, prayer has remained somewhat of a mystery to me.

I have no doubt that my praying, over the years, has not been a waste of time. I believe that any sincere attempt to be personal with God is honored by him. At the same time, I have often felt so inadequate in my attempts.

As I have tried to understand prayer more fully, I have focused on its various aspects - praise and adoration, thanksgiving, confession, petition, and intercession. I have tried to understand and practice the processes that others have suggested would be helpful - things like picking an appropriate and consistent time of day, keeping a journal, memorizing scripture, using a prayer list and so on. I have tried to understand the theological elements of prayer, such as repentance and worship, which make praying a viable process. And all of these things have been good and helpful.

Still I have struggled. Techniques and research are great as tools, but the act of praying, itself, is not an object to simply be understood and manipulated. It is a conversation. What I have come to understand is that my need is not so much to learn more about prayer, but to actually get at the *act* of praying. We do not need an academic understanding of prayer nearly as much as we need to learn how to stand in the presence of God and have a conversation with him.

Of course we do engage our minds in the praying process, and that is why it is helpful to understand all of the things mentioned above. We also engage our emotions. That's why we sometimes feel that our praying is ineffective - we don't "feel" the presence of God. There is a third element that we don't often consider. We also have to engage our bodies. We exist in a physical environment and have to use our bodies in all that we do.

But, while all of our physical parts are engaged in the process of praying, the essence of praying is spiritual. It is communication with God. Communication is not an emotional, physical or mental activity, it is spiritual. The most important thing is to engage our spirit.

And that is what this book is about. How do we get into an ongoing conversation with God so that we are engaged with him in a vibrant and powerful way? How can we engage our physical parts (emotions, body and mind) so that we "feel" like we are interacting with him? And what distinctions should we make so that we don't confuse the physical experiences with the actual spiritual interaction?

The purpose of this book is to demystify and clarify the experience of praying. It is to help you personally engage in an ongoing conversation with God. It is to help you experience such a vibrant and powerful interaction with God that your spiritual life will come alive in ways you have never experienced before. It is to direct your attention away from the ***process of prayer*** and toward the ***personal activity of praying***. Only when you achieve these purposes will praying become the exciting conversation that will deepen your relationship with God and cause you to have deep joy in your interaction with him.

But before we go on, let me just cut to the chase. Praying is not for wimps! It is not that anyone is excluded from being effective in praying. It is just that anyone who is serious about being effective is going to have to put aside any ideas that praying is just saying a few words and asking God for stuff. It is, instead, the communication that takes place in the spiritual arena, in the midst of a spiritual war. It requires commitment, determination, persistence, an understanding of purpose and, most of all, a deep love that is strong enough to keep you on track.

My desired outcome for this book is for every reader to move beyond an intellectual understanding of prayer, to a continual personal interaction with God. To help this process along, I have designed a methodology for you to take advantage of. Each chapter contains an information base to help you understand the relational concepts of praying. You will also find my own musings about how I have come to experience the praying process. Then, at the end of each chapter, you will find specific suggestions and questions to help you take the information and apply it to life.

Let me suggest that you will find this book more helpful if you use it as a resource over a long period of time. The first time you might simply want to read the book through, from beginning to end, and become familiar with all of the ideas. Then, go through it again using the suggestions to develop your praying.

Now, if you are ready to learn to engage in praying that goes beyond the "wimpish," hold on tight and read on. This could change your spiritual life forever.

I don't, specifically, remember the day that I decided to try and take my relationship with God to the next level. It has been a growing and evolving experience for me. I have always wanted to know God more deeply, but I have learned that it is not something that just happens because I want it to. It began happening for me when I started pursuing it as a lifestyle.

The place in my life where the relationship has become most evident is in my praying. I no longer say prayers. I envision that to be like bundling up a package and throwing it on the back of a transport truck to be carried to God.

Now, when interacting with God, I actually stand in his presence. It is the difference in being personal and impersonal. I now work alongside him as an apprentice, rather than having a life separate from his presence. Now, instead of just sending him messages to help me or tell me what to do, we have staff meetings and private training sessions to hammer things out.

I still don't know how it all works. My ability to interact at deeper and deeper levels is still growing. I don't believe there is any end to the growth possibilities.

I have been able to take this road because I decided, decisively, that it was the path I would follow for my life. Anyone who wants to have that kind of relationship with God will have to make the same decision and begin the journey without looking back.

Chapter 1

Moving Beyond Prayer Games

What is Prayer?

I have been going to church for longer than I can remember. My parents were both Christians and actively involved in all facets of church life. If the doors were open, our family was there. If the doors weren't open, they had a key to get in.

Overall, I recall good experiences in church while growing up. But as I got older and involved in more adult activities, I remember one aspect of church life that I never cared that much for - prayer meeting. For some reason that always seemed uninteresting to me. I remember that, after a couple of songs and a sermon, or Bible lesson, we would have a time of prayer. Now, the singing and Bible times were OK, but that prayer time? B-o-r-i-n-g!

Over the years I have tried to decipher what made it so unappealing to me, and I think I have figured it out. Prayer is so personal! No, not just personal. I mean really, really personal! To make prayer have real meaning, a person has to actually take the time, and make the effort, to experience the presence of God, **at that moment**. You can sing songs and just enjoy the music. You can listen to a person open up the scriptures and appreciate the new knowledge you gain. But praying is different. You have to engage God at a deep, personal level, and that means having your own life lined up with him. It means that you make his purpose to be your purpose, without having any deliberate sin going on in your life. Being that personal with God requires the very deepest commitment, sacrifice and love. And frankly, most people just are not there. When I find praying unappealing and difficult, these are exactly the issues I find myself struggling with.

Jesus once told the story of two men who felt the need to lift a prayer up to God. One was a powerful religious leader. When he stood before God to pray, he was full of confidence. All of his life had been devoted to studying God's law, and he knew all the "dos and don'ts" of the religion. Being the faithful adherent that he was, he was also very diligent in following the letter of the law to the highest degree possible. So, when he began to pray, he started by thanking God that he was not like one of the "low life" sinners that were all around, and that he was a righteous man who deserved to be one of the chosen of God.

The other man was a tax collector. This was the kind of "low life" that the religious leader was talking about. It seems this guy was feeling pretty down on himself. He had been a dishonest man for many years. He went out of his way to overcharge people's tax bills in order to enrich himself. He even worked for the occupying Roman government that kept his own people in bondage. As he stood before God he was in spiritual anguish and would not even lift his face toward heaven. He simply cried out to God, "Have mercy on me for my horrible sins."

In telling this story, Jesus made a shocking judgment about the praying of the two men. He said that it was the "low life" tax collector that God listened to, rather than the "righteous" religious leader. Then he gave the reason for his pronouncement.

It seems that the religious leader thought so highly of himself that he believed he could enter God's presence because of his own goodness. He couldn't see the offenses in his own life and how he displeased God, so he felt no need to repent. He didn't see a need to engage God personally and accommodate God's way.

The tax collector, on the other hand, recognized his defects and bowed his heart toward God. He acknowledged his separation from God and yielded his heart in repentance. He did what was necessary to pull himself into the very presence of God.

Typically, we think of prayer as a ritual to go through or as a time to tell God our wants and woes. But that is only part of the picture. That aspect of prayer is certainly important, but does not give us a full picture of what is going on. In Hebrews 10:22, the writer gives us what I believe is a more complete description. He writes, "Let us draw near to God with a sincere heart in full assurance of faith, having our hearts sprinkled to cleanse us from a guilty conscience and having our bodies washed with pure water."

The important phrase in this passage is "draw near to God." This is where the religious leader and the tax collector parted company. One only spoke words, the other did what was necessary to enter God's presence. This is also the reason that the praying portion of prayer meeting can seem so dry.

So, exactly what does the writer mean when he says "draw near to God?" It refers to the individual who *steps into the very presence of God*. It is about intimacy. Think of a person in your life that you see virtually every day but don't really like. You are not spiritually connected with that person and don't sense any personal bond with them. It is possible to be physically next to someone yet not be near them spiritually. It is also possible to be spiritually connected with someone who is thousands of miles away. You have someone, like a parent or spouse or child or dear friend, in your life, that you have that kind of deep relationship with. You experience that intimacy whether they are physically present or not.

God is not a human being, but he is a spiritual person. And it is spiritual individuals who are able to interact with each other on a spiritual level. As spiritual beings ourselves, we are able to connect not only with other humans, but also with God.

So let's cut to the chase. What is "prayer," anyway? In our innermost being we sense what it is. It is talking to God, right? Well, sure that's what it is. But as we think more deeply, there is another question that emerges. What does "talk to God" mean?

In order to answer that question, we need to know who God is, who we are, and what kind of options we have as we talk. We will actually get to all of that, but first let's take a moment to ponder this on a general level.

The most important thing we need to understand about praying is that it is not about getting things, and it is not about talking - it is about relating! Answers to prayer are not things we get, they are touches of God! In its essence, prayer is a conversation - but it is a special kind of conversation. It is possible for us to use conversation-like processes in a lot of places that are not really conversations. For instance, can you have a conversation with the tree out in your back yard? Well, you can go stand in front of it and start talking, but it cannot respond back. You can let words flow forth, but there is no conversation.

How about with the squirrel up in the tree? It is a living thing and can pay attention to you. But if you talk to it, can you get a conversation going? I don't think so. No personal relationship has been, or even can be, formed.

So, how about your pet dog? It will not only pay attention to what you say, but will give back affection. Does that mean that you can have a conversation with it? Well, no! To begin with, your dog can't understand what you are saying, and even when it responds it is not to your thoughts and ideas, but to the affection or the training you have given it.

Conversation requires another individual who can understand your thoughts, words, ideas and feelings, and can respond back to you in a rational, willful and self-conscious way. This kind of conversation can only take place with another being who has a spiritual capacity.

So, how about "prayer?" Prayer is a conversation, but not just any conversation. We can converse with ourselves, but that is not prayer. We can converse with other human individuals, but that is not prayer, either. "Prayer" is a word that we reserve only for our conversation with God.

There is a problem, though, that we typically encounter when we think about prayer. A conversation goes two ways. The verse above says we are to "draw near to God." "Drawing near" creates a two-way interaction. But, when was the last time you engaged God in a two-way conversation? I have read lots of books on prayer and have listened to a lot of people talk about it. Almost everyone advocates this two-way communication, but it is hard to find much instruction about how to actually do it because so much of what we read primarily emphasizes the human side of praying.

What are the aspects of prayer that you are aware of? Praise, thanksgiving, petition, confession. . . ? For the most part, these things are only half a conversation - that half where *we* do the talking. But a conversation requires that we be talked to, as well. How do we get that part?

Prayer is, indeed, a conversation. But if we are truly going to pray, we will have to learn how to engage in a real conversation that goes beyond what we normally conceive. That's why prayer meeting time is often so difficult. Although we know the right vocabulary and sentence structure to put together a pretty decent prayer, too many times we end up simply voicing empty words.

I believe that praying is about the hardest thing to learn in a foreign language - not because of the vocabulary, but because of the deep desire to be personal and spontaneous at time when you are not fluent enough to do it. When I was living in Japan and learning the Japanese language, I clearly remember the time when my language instructor began teaching me to pray.

The teacher was great, though. He had developed a system for teaching us how to pray. There are particular words and phrases that are common in prayer language. He simply taught us the common phrases, then all we had to do was to substitute different words to make it into a nice sounding prayer. For instance, he taught us how to say, "Lord, thank you for . . . " Then we could tack on whatever we wanted to express thanks for - church, family, health, etc.

But especially in the beginning, I had to plan out everything I wanted to say in advance. At that stage in my language learning, my public prayers were more like a speech than a conversation - and it didn't really feel like I was praying. Whether in another language or in our own native tongue, if we don't dig down deep within our being and make our words express the actual intent of our heart, the expressions don't qualify as prayer because no communication is taking place.

We are actually at a bit of a disadvantage when it comes to prayer. In other conversations our interaction is with a physical/tangible being, and we can get feedback with our physical senses. But in prayer we are talking with a person who is pure spirit. The conversation is in an entirely different arena. As spiritual beings, we humans are capable of communicating at that level, but it doesn't come naturally or easily. First, we have to learn how our spiritual part operates. Then we have to make a concerted effort to develop our sensitivities in that arena.

Prayer is a conversation with God - a real conversation with a real person, at a level that penetrates to the very core of who we are. And that is what we are going to try and get at in this journey.

So recognize, right now, that you are about to take a step that goes to the very core of your being. Taking this step will require that you step into spiritual territory that makes you more vulnerable than any other activity you will ever do in your life. A wimp simply can't do this! So just how can we learn to "draw near to God" in the realm of pure spirit?

Digging Deeper

- Take time to imagine, in your mind, what an ideal conversation with God would be like. If you find this difficult, think of a person that you have had a deep spiritual connection with, then imagine having that same kind of personal spiritual intimacy with God. What would it be like?

- Take about five minutes, right now, to see how personal you can get with God.

God is a being who exists in a form, and in a realm, that is way beyond human understanding. Because of that, I found myself struggling to figure him out.

I realize that, ultimately, God has to be known by faith. But there also has to be some basis for the faith. I have done a lot of research and a lot of soul searching to develop that foundational understanding for my life.

Many people try to come to their own understanding about God without having a basis for their conclusions. They may be able to discern some spiritual truth, but will never get at a relationship with God on their own.

The Bible is the only revelation of God which gives us specific insight into him as a person. With that knowledge, I found, for myself, a way to get at developing a relationship with God. I discovered two steps I have to continually take to know him more.

The first is research. This doesn't seem spiritual, but, since we live in physical reality, there is no way around the necessity to gain a knowledge base. I had to, personally, take the time to research the Bible to try and understand God more.

The second step is spiritual. I have to take the time and effort to meditate and ponder the implications of his revelation. It is here that I learned to touch God. My due diligence has not just convinced me, but has brought me to a deep and intimate interaction with him.

Anyone who wants to know God in a personal relationship will have to do the same thing I did. My knowledge may be able to point you in the right direction, but it will never be a substitute for your own due diligence.

Chapter 2
Understanding the Unique Qualities of God

One day while I was living in Japan, I was walking down the street with a Japanese friend of mine. We were talking about a mutual friend and he pulled out a picture with that person in it. I thought it was a great picture and enthusiastically told him so. When he saw how much I liked it, he offered to give it to me. Dumb American that I was, I immediately accepted it from him. But when I looked at his face, it was as if he had just lost his best friend. It became obvious to me, very quickly, that there was something else going on here. He had offered the picture as a gesture of kindness, but I, obviously, was not supposed to accept it from him.

Japanese culture has some ways of doing things that are different from American culture. When he offered the picture, the proper response would have been to politely refuse it. If he had really wanted me to have it, he would have offered it at least two more times.

Fortunately, I recognized the problem quickly and didn't take it. But I learned a very important lesson that day. If you want to effectively communicate with someone, you had better understand their culture.

There are two players in the game of prayer. The first one is God. In order to effectively interact with him, we have to understand who he is and what he is like.

The second player is the human individual. We have to understand the same thing here. The nature of any communication is dependent on the people who are doing the communicating.

For instance, if you wanted to communicate with a Spanish person in Spain, how would you do it? First, you would have to make contact with the individual - whether in person or with some kind of communication device. Next, you would need to convey a message and receive messages that are sent back. There are other factors to consider, as well, such as what language you will use, what other kind of interference might present itself, and so on.

The point is, successful communication depends on understanding both the situation and the individuals involved in the process. I cannot speak to the Spaniard who is in Spain in the same way that I would speak to my wife who is here with me. For one thing, I don't speak Spanish. There are differences that must be taken into account in order to communicate effectively.

The same is true when we want to communicate with God. He operates in a certain arena and communicates in particular ways. If we don't understand who he is and how he operates, we will never be able to engage him effectively. So, let's understand more about God's role as a player in the process of praying.

Who is God?

To begin with, if we want to relate personally to God, we have to think of him in terms of a "who," not a "what." Relationship involves one self-aware individual interacting with another who can relate back. God is not some kind of spiritual plasma, or some unknowable being way out in the cosmos. He is a personal individual who we are able to engage in an intimate relationship.

It is, certainly, true that God is ultimately beyond our full understanding, as long as we are confined to the material universe. But that is only part of the picture. While it may be true that we cannot know him fully, God has sufficiently revealed himself to us so that we may know him enough to have a relationship with him. In 1 John 5:20, we read, "We know also that the Son of God has come and has given us understanding, so that we may know him who is true. And we are in him who is true - even in his Son Jesus Christ. He is the true God and eternal life."

Notice that the verse says we can "know him" - not just know who he is or know about him. This is very personal language. And it goes even further. It says, "we are in him." Talk about personal! What this means is, we belong to him and have somehow been united with him. This allows us the most intimate kind of interaction.

Frankly, most people don't normally think of God as a person in the same way they think of a human being as one. That being said, this "normal" way of thinking about God is the complete opposite of reality. Even though he exists in a form that is different from physical humanity, he is a person.

God is Spiritual

The reason most of us don't think of God as a person is because we tend to use humanity as the standard for defining personhood. But the truth is the reverse. God is the standard for defining personhood. God is not a person because *we* are, we are people because *God* is. We do not create God in our image, he created us in his.

This does not mean that he is flesh and blood the way we, mortals, are. No, personhood is a spiritual concept. It is spiritual characteristics that make up the essence of a person. So, if we want to understand what a person is like, we have to understand those essential spiritual characteristics. Let's take a moment and look at the basic characteristics of God so that we can begin to see the channels within which our communication must take place.

God is Spirit

The first characteristic of a spiritual being is to be spirit. John 4:24 talks about this characteristic of God. It tells us, "God is spirit, and his worshipers must worship in spirit and in truth."

What this means is that God's essence is something other than physical or material. We can go up to our friends and touch them, hear their actual voice, smell their fragrance (a pleasant one, I hope), see their face and taste their skin (actually probably not a good idea in most situations, but we could do it). In other words, human relationships are able to engage the physical senses.

Since God is not a material being in the same way humans are, we cannot engage him that way. This does not mean, though, that he is not real, just that he exists in a form that requires us to engage him spiritually, not physically.

God Has Knowledge

A second characteristic of a spiritual being is the ability to have knowledge. Acquiring and using knowledge is a self-conscious activity. It involves more than just having facts stored in the brain or being able to react automatically to a situation. Rather, it requires that an individual be able to accumulate information and interpret it based on a broader context.

God has this kind of knowledge, only he has it in the ultimate sense. In John 3:20, is written, "For God is greater than our hearts, and he knows everything." He is able to evaluate what is going on in every part of reality and determine how to use that knowledge most effectively.

God Has Creativity

The third characteristic of a spiritual being is creativity. To be creative means that a person can conceive of something that does not presently exist and bring it into being. We typically think of this in terms of the arts or technology. Most of the creativity that we, as humans, generate are adaptations of things that already exist.

God, though, is able to operate at an entirely different level. He can conceive of things that don't even exist and bring them into being. Certainly one of the most well known verses in the Bible refers to this creative capacity of God. Genesis 1:1 speaks of God's creative activity as he spoke into existence the material universe. There we read, "In the beginning God created the heavens and the earth." As we continue on through the first three chapters of Genesis, we get even more detail about his creative capacity.

God Has Personality

The next characteristic of a spiritual being is personality. Personality reflects an individual's uniqueness. Every spiritual being is a "one-of-a-kind" unique creation. Personality, though, goes way beyond mere uniqueness. In one way we can look at our pets, or even snowflakes, and point to a type of uniqueness. The uniqueness of non-spiritual entities relates strictly to genetics or mechanical structure. But personality, as it relates to spiritual beings, requires self-consciousness. This uniqueness allows us to take our basic personality and make deliberate changes.

God is not restricted, in any way, by DNA or mechanical structure. He is a unique individual who can decide what kind of being he will be and can make decisions, on the fly, as to how he will display his personality in his relationships with others. Understanding the full essence of God's personality is beyond our ability. But we can know some things based on his acts, his revelation and the way he interacts with mankind. All of the acts that he performs are expressions of his unique personality. There is not just one single scripture passage that we can point to which encapsulates his personality. Yet we do see how it is expressed every time we read, in Scripture, about his goodness and love, mercy, hatred of evil and his grace.

God Has Free Will

The fifth characteristic of a spiritual being is free will. This is displayed in humans by the fact that individuals are able to decide what to do and how to react to life situations.

God, being the ultimate spiritual being in all of existence, has the ability to decide for himself how everything will operate. He chose what to create, how it would operate and has the ability to make sure that everything works the way he wants it to.

In Ephesians 1:4-5, we are told, "For he chose us in him before the creation of the world to be holy and blameless in his sight. In love he predestined us to be adopted as his sons through Jesus Christ, in accordance with his pleasure and will." All of the things in these verses were an exercise of God's free will - his choosing of humanity to live in relationship with himself, as well as the option to allow mankind to also exercise free will.

God is Male and Female

Another characteristic of spiritual beings are the attributes related to being male or female. In this case, gender is not merely a reference to the physical differences of individuals. An actual spiritual difference exists between the genders of human beings. In humanity this plays out in a particular way (and we will look at that later when we discuss the spiritual characteristics of humans).

God created mankind so that each gender only contained a portion of a whole. In Genesis 2:24, we read, "For this reason a man will leave his father and mother and be united to his wife, and they will become one flesh." This whole idea of "one flesh" signifies the combining of two beings to create a particular kind of unity. It is only in the coming together of two people in marriage that the whole is completed.

God, however, has all of the characteristics of that aspect of spirituality within himself. God is a unity in and of himself. In Deuteronomy 6:4 it is written, "Hear, O Israel: The LORD our God, the LORD is one."

God is Eternal

The seventh characteristic of a spiritual being is eternalness. Humanity, in general, was created at a certain point in time, and each individual human was also created at a particular moment. But from the moment of that creation, the individual becomes eternal and will never cease to exist.

God is eternal in a different way. There never was a time when he didn't exist, and he will always continue to exist into the future. John 5:26 tells us, "For as the Father has life in himself, so he has granted the Son to have life in himself." This idea of "life in himself" means that his existence is not derived from any other being.

God Has Dominion

The eighth characteristic is dominion. Dominion is the trait that allows for control and ownership. An individual human is able to have control over such things as property, environment, relationship interactions and many other things. Ownership is also possible, but only in a limited sort of way.

God, however, is able to have dominion over all things in an ultimate way. He is the creator and sustainer of everything that exists and is able to determine the ultimate destiny of every part of the universal order. We read in 1 Chronicles 29:11, "Yours, O LORD, is the greatness and the power and the glory and the majesty and the splendor, for everything in heaven and earth is yours. Yours, O LORD, is the kingdom; you are exalted as head over all."

God is Self-Conscious

The final characteristic that we will consider here is self-consciousness. This is the characteristic which allows an individual to be aware of self. It is the one that allows people to make personal evaluations and to generate intentional actions which affect life direction.

God is the center point of everything that exists. In Exodus 3:13-14, Moses asked God to identify himself in a way that would give him credibility before the people of Israel. God answered back with an expression that put to the forefront his self-existence. Moses said to God, "Suppose I go to the Israelites and say to them, 'The God of your fathers has sent me to you,' and they ask me, 'What is his name?' Then what shall I tell them?" God said to Moses, "I AM WHO I AM. This is what you are to say to the Israelites: 'I AM has sent me to you.'" Not only is God the center point, he is also aware of his position, and he has designed all that happens specifically to operate around him as the focus.

God is Objective

People conceive of God in a lot of different ways. Some see him as some kind of unknowable blob, a ghostly figure, the sum total of everything or even an imaginary creature that helps us get through hard times. Regardless of the specific image, for many people the underlying thought is that God is something subjective. He is something they feel, or someone they hope is there when they need to call on him, or some unknowable being that started the universe up and just lets it run.

But nothing could be further from the truth. God is not some nebulous being that cannot be defined. He is not just something out there that we have to try and sense with our emotions or tune into with some kind of ESP. He is an objective being who dwells in a portion of reality that is outside of the physical universe, but who is able to freely interact within the material universe, as well.

He is not less real just because we can't experience him physically. In fact, the most real part of existence is that part of reality where God is - the eternal place. It was here before the physical universe existed and will be here long after it is gone. That spiritual part of reality is profoundly real, and material reality, as we know and experience it, is but a unique and temporary portion of it. It was created to serve a specific purpose of God.

The fact is, God is an objective being. He exists as a person who can know and be known. The person who believes that God is a cloud or blob or a figment of someone's imagination, will not even attempt to explore more deeply and to understand the personal side of who he is and what he is really like. It is only when an individual is able to grasp the fact that God is a real and objective being that it becomes possible to begin exploring who he really is.

God is personal

Perhaps the most profound thing that we must understand about God is that he is a person, and he is personal. He is a real objective being who attempts to engage us on a conscious and personal level. Some people think it kind of odd to refer to God as a person, but personhood is actually the essence of his being.

The Bible tells us that when God created mankind, he made us in his image. Now certainly this does not mean that we physically look like him. The image of God is a spiritual concept and refers to the characteristics mentioned above - things such as self-consciousness, free will, personality, and the like. So when God created mankind with these characteristics, he essentially created a "person" who was like himself. God is not a person because we are people. We are people because he is a person, and he created us to be like himself.

The result of this is that it becomes possible for him to interact with human individuals, since the essential spiritual components that are in God, and which are necessary for communication and intimacy, are also in mankind.

It is actually the most logical thing imaginable for this to be so. As we read the Bible there are many, many attempts to describe what he is like. A large number of the representations are anthropomorphisms - ascribing human properties to God. We read such things as "the eyes of the Lord are on the righteous" (1 Pet. 3:12) or "like the voice of the Almighty" (Ezekiel 1:24). These expressions are used because they convey to us the personal nature of God, who is actively and personally engaged with us.

Physical reality is essentially a limited part of a greater spiritual reality. It only makes sense that the way we experience reality in the physical world would have a more profound counterpart in that part of reality that is beyond us. It is obvious that human beings are able to experience personal interaction with other humans. The extension of that truth is that God made it so that we can also reach beyond the veil of eternity to experience that same kind of personal spiritual interaction with him.

God is purposeful

It may seem rather presumptuous for human beings to claim knowledge of the purposes of God. And that would be true except for one fact. He has revealed to mankind at least a portion of what his purposes are.

When it comes to understanding why God created the physical order and put mankind in it, the bottom line is that he did it to develop a class of beings that he could have a personal relationship with. God, certainly, has other purposes in his spiritual economy that only he knows about. We can get a glimpse of some of God's purposes in verses such as Ephesians 1:9-10, where it speaks of God's revelation of his purpose to mankind.

There it is written, "And he made known to us the mystery of his will according to his good pleasure, which he purposed in Christ, to be put into effect when the times will have reached their fulfillment - to bring all things in heaven and on earth together under one head, even Christ."

But his primary purpose for mankind is relationship. In John 3:16-18, he spells it out quite clearly. It says, "For God so loved the world that he gave his one and only Son, that whoever believes in him shall not perish but have eternal life. For God did not send his Son into the world to condemn the world, but to save the world through him. Whoever believes in him is not condemned, but whoever does not believe stands condemned already because he has not believed in the name of God's one and only Son."

God put mankind on earth in a particular kind of environment in order to test and develop us. The ultimate purpose of our experience is to voluntarily choose to enter into a personal relationship with God. Whether or not individuals actually choose that, though, is a matter of their own personal decisions.

Who, Indeed, Is God?

It seems that God is a social person. He longed for a class of beings who were like himself and with whom he could have intimate, personal contact. An important aspect of intimacy is that it must be consensual - all parties must willingly give themselves to it.

God could have made robots that would obey his every whim. But you can't have a relationship with a robot. Relationship requires a self-conscious being who willingly enters into the interaction - a being like God himself. So God created such beings - mankind. He put us in an environment where we can make free choices about whether or not to engage him. Ultimately, God will lift those who choose to enter a relationship with him to that part of eternity where they will dwell with him through the rest of eternity. Those who do not make this choice will be released to live out their eternity outside of that eternal relationship with him.

Digging Deeper

- Take some time to think deeply about what God is like. Do you conceive of him as personal or impersonal? Do you find yourself able to think of him as someone you can relate to very intimately, or do you find that kind of thinking to be difficult?

- If you struggle with this, take the time to consider more deeply the ideas that are in this chapter so you can come to some resolution about it.

When it comes to personal relationships, I don't think I am much different than most people. I want close personal friendships - where I am able to establish a "soul mate" type connection.

Out of the hundreds of people I know, I believe that I only have three or four people who fit into that category. According to the experts, that is about average. To achieve that level of intimacy, we have to trust the other person so highly that we are willing to be completely vulnerable. I treasure those relationships, but even with that kind of closeness it is not easy. It takes a lot of work to maintain it.

This is where I want to be with God, too. It is especially hard with God because he is so morally perfect. I feel inadequate and inferior in his presence. I don't want him seeing my weaknesses.

I had to make a choice. He said he loves me, and I have had to be willing to take him at his word and trust that he will not take my weaknesses and use them against me.

When I have interacted with him, he has always proven himself trustworthy. He does point out my weaknesses, but only for the purpose of teaching me to overcome them. He then pours his love over me so that I can experience his power and mercy.

Some things are beyond my ability to express in words. My relationship with God is one of those things. But it exists and continues to grow deeper and deeper as I interact with him.

Chapter 3
Why We Can Connect With God

The more I write the more addicted I get to writing. I think it has a lot to do with the things I am writing about. When I write about personal development and spiritual growth, I have to do a lot of research and personal contemplation. I don't necessarily like the research part, but the insights I gain into the topics I write about are profound and exciting - at least to me.

This has been especially true as I have thought about my own life. I am sometimes amazed at how much I know about myself on a surface level that doesn't translate to deep down knowledge. It would seem logical that I would have more insight into my own life than almost anything else, since I live inside of my skin. But the truth is, my ways are so familiar, and my living habits so pervasive, that I don't actually think much about them - that is until there is some compelling reason to do so.

For instance, I recently decided to spin off one of my businesses. I had done that business for several years and actually enjoyed it. It also fit with other things that I was doing. But I found myself frustrated - not because I didn't like doing the work, but because there were other things I would rather do with my time. It actually took me quite a while to search my heart and figure out exactly what the frustration was.

That same dynamic is one reason why public worship is so important for each of us. When we hear a sermon, or Bible lesson, it forces us to think more deeply than usual about issues outside of our regular box. Writing does that same thing for me, and the more I do it the more I enjoy it.

Think about yourself, for a moment. Why do you have the job you have? Why do you watch that certain TV show that is your favorite? Why do you read the kinds of books that you read?

Now, if you just skipped over these questions without stopping to try and discern your actual inner motives, you are probably treating these issues like you treat most of the rest of your life. Typically, we just don't think deeply about life issues. It is not a horrible sin if you don't do it a lot, but you will never really know much about yourself unless you do.

Let me take it one step further. If you want to have a deep relationship with God, the better you know yourself, the greater the relationship possibilities. Let's take a moment to explore what we are like under our skin.

Who are Humans?

It is essential to have an understanding of who God is so that we can understand who we are praying to. But a relationship that uses prayer as a communication medium requires two parties. Having looked at the "God half" of the relationship in the previous chapter, we now turn our attention to the human side.

Human beings are a special creation of God. There are many other creatures that are a part of the material reality we live in, but humans are unique. We are the only beings in the created order who have a spiritual capacity. Other creatures have physical characteristics which allow them to live a life on earth, but they don't have the spiritual characteristics of the image of God. Other creatures are bound by their genetic code to live a particular kind of existence. Humans, certainly, have predispositions based on genetics, but we also have a special ability to override our genetic inclinations and decide for ourselves how we will move into the future.

It is not necessary, here, to go into a long discussion about the nature of humanity because so many of the important ideas were touched on above in the discussion about the nature of God. But for the sake of completeness, let's briefly look at some of the special characteristics that make up humankind.

Humans are created beings

As was mentioned above, God had a desire for personal interaction and created mankind to fulfill that purpose. Whereas God, himself, is eternal and there never was a time when he did not exist, mankind had a beginning. Each human spirit is a new act of creation by God. In this earthly environment, every time a child is conceived, God creates a spirit that is tied to that new human. The physical body is designed to live in material reality for a finite period of time, then it dies. The spirit, however, is eternal from the moment of its creation.

Humans are spiritual beings created in the image of God

The discussion of God, above, listed a number of characteristics which define the essence of God's personhood. These characteristics are all spiritual qualities which make him the kind of being he is. Humanity was created in the image of God. This is not a reference to physical appearance. When God created mankind in his own image, he put in us the very characteristics of his personhood. This includes the things mentioned above - spirit, knowledge, creativity, personality, male and female, eternalness, dominion, free will and self-consciousness.

Of course, we cannot experience these spiritual characteristics to the extent that God does because he is still a higher being than we are. On top of that, we are specifically limited as long as we are confined to the physical realm.

Still, as spiritual beings, we are able to exercise the spiritual part of ourselves in some very powerful ways. We are able to express it in all of the relationships that we are engaged in - our relationship with ourselves, with other human beings and with God.

Humans are personal beings

The ability to be intimate is the bottom line of spiritual interaction. God, himself, is personal and created mankind for the express purpose of having a partner to interact with.

This kind of intimacy is not possible between beings who are less than personal. It is possible to enjoy the services of a robot, but it is impossible to be personal with it. It is possible to enjoy the companionship of a pet, but your dog or cat does not have the capacity for personal intimacy.

Intimacy requires self-conscious persons who are able to deliberately and purposefully give of themselves. God created humans to be personal like himself and to be able to connect on a spiritual level spirit to spirit.

Interacting Spirit to Spirit

The interactions that individuals have with self, other people and with God are spiritual interactions. It is possible for humans to have a physical relationship with other human beings, but the essence, of even that relationship, is spiritual. The relationship that an individual has with God is purely spiritual.

We can have that spirit-to-spirit interaction with God, but we must first establish a relationship with him. Without this relationship, praying is not possible. Just because a person is able to throw out words in the form of sentences addressed to God, does not mean that actual communication is taking place. We can say sentences to a wall, for that matter. Communication requires a personal connection.

The essence of personal interaction with God has to do with who he is and who we are. Let's summarize the operation of spiritual communication between a person and God.

- In the beginning God existed in spiritual reality. At that point material reality did not exist. [1]
- God came to desire a creature he could personally interact with - one who had the same spiritual characteristics as himself so he could interact in a true love relationship. [2]
- God created material existence as a place to establish this creature. In this environment these created beings decide whether or not they want to have an intimate relationship with God. [3]
- God, himself, established the terms of the relationship. It is one in which mankind must deliberately choose to establish a relationship with God and to live a life that is consistent with the nature of God's reality. [4]
- Mankind is completely incapable of measuring up to the standard God requires for this relationship to exist. [5]
- So he made a way for humans to overcome the problem by the sacrificial death, and the resurrection, of Jesus Christ. [6]
- Individuals choose for themselves whether or not to enter this relationship. [7]
- Those who choose to relate to God will spend eternity in personal relationship with him. [8]
- Those who choose not to relate to God will have their choice honored and spend eternity in a separate part of the eternal realm which is outside of God's presence. [9]

The individuals who are necessary to make up a spiritual relationship exist. The mechanism for interacting also exists. Because of this, both God and individual human beings are capable of connecting with each other on a spiritual level.

The only thing left is for the relationship to actually be established and developed. God, from his side, is perfectly poised at every moment to allow the relationship to operate. The determining factor, as to whether or not it actually happens, lies in the hands of individual human beings. We have to make a deliberate choice that we want the relationship. But that, alone, is not enough. We have to ask for it, then operate within it. Once the relationship is established and working, we are then able to explore the full reality of intimacy with God. At that point praying becomes possible.

Digging Deeper

- What have you done, specifically, to establish a relationship with God? How do you know that the relationship actually exists?

- Think about yourself as a spiritual being. What have you done to make it possible to personally interact with God?

- Take 15 minutes, right now, to explore what you need to do to connect more deeply with God.

My personal breakthrough with praying came when my paradigm regarding the nature of prayer did a complete shift. And I don't believe that my experience is unique.

I grew up in church where prayer was a common topic of discussion and of study. I always wanted to be closer to God, so I even read and researched on my own to learn more. One of the things that was always taught, in all of the resources I studied, was that praying was talking to God. But when it got to the point of teaching "how to do it" there was always a step by step formula.

I don't know that you can get around the need for that. It is a fact that there are elements of praying that can be identified and taught. The problem is not the formula, but the level of understanding of the person using it.

One day I actually experienced the conversation I was having with God as a personal conversation with him, rather than as a formula to work through. Once I experienced that, I was never satisfied with working through a formula again. I always wanted the personal touch with God.

I still want that and am determined to have it. Now, even though I use the categories of the formula, I never think in those terms. I simply talk to God.

Chapter 4
Praying is More Than a Formula
How to Experience the Different Elements of Prayer

There is a particular nutritional supplement that I used to take that is in capsule form. The capsule itself is made of some kind of gelatin that simply dissolves when the pill is swallowed. When the capsule dissolves, the nutrients inside are then able to enter into a person's system and do their work.

It should never happen, but once in a while, when I opened the bottle, I would find a defective capsule. It was put together as it should be, but there was nothing inside. It would not harm me to take one of these capsules, but there was nothing in it to do me any good, either.

In my life I have experienced prayer in the same way - like an empty capsule. I have focused on the form and said all of the right words, but not had it filled with any content from my heart - as if the words themselves were something substantive. It tends to happen at times when I know I need to pray but do not make the effort to step into the presence of God. It happens sometimes when saying the blessing at a meal or in a Sunday School class or in other places where prayer has become routine.

The fact is, words only have meaning within a relationship if they express real meaning from our inner core. It is not mere words, but the expression of self that is able to transcend our physical limitations and cross over into the eternal spiritual sphere.

Sometimes it is hard to get at the true nature of praying in real life because we see it as more of a formula than a conversation. While God is a real person, and most believers acknowledge that fact intellectually, actually experiencing God as a person is not something that comes naturally. Our physical existence is the most easily accessible part of our lives, so our tendency is to try and tap into a relationship with God using our senses. The result is that we often think of prayer more as a formula than as a conversation with a real person.

Anyone who has ever read books on prayer will recognize the most common elements of the formula. It typically consists of 1) praise and adoration, 2) thanksgiving, 3) intercession, 4) petition and 5) confession. Now there is certainly nothing wrong with these elements of prayer. In fact, it is virtually impossible to engage God without using these categories of conversation.

But prayer is not simply a matter of taking a list of conversation categories and filling in the blanks. That would be like sitting down with a close friend, or your spouse, with a list of conversation topics every time you got together to talk. When was the last time you did that? Typically, you engage other people on a more spontaneous and immediate level. You talk about the things you really care about.

And that's the way it ought to be when we converse with God. We need to talk to him about a lot more than the five things mentioned above. When we limit ourselves to those five categories, we are not really having a conversation. We are simply working our way through a formula.

There is another problem that exists with "the formula" as well. All of these elements go only one way - from us to God. A conversation requires two-way communication. Not only do we have to learn to talk to God, we have to learn to listen to him, as well.

To understand this dialogue more fully, I decided to work my way though the Bible and see what kind of conversation topics I found as people engaged God in prayer. Certainly the five above are prominent so I will start with them. But I found others, as well, that show us a bigger picture. We need to understand how far beyond "formula" a conversation with God can go.

Praise and Adoration [1]

In Ephesians 3:20-21, it says, "Now to him who is able to do immeasurably more than all we ask or imagine, according to his power that is at work within us, to him be glory in the church and in Christ Jesus throughout all generations, for ever and ever! Amen." Praise and adoration simply means to tell someone how wonderful they are. You have people you respect and love. It is very natural that you express that to them. The more love and respect you feel in your heart toward someone, the more praise and adoration you want to heap on them.

A lot of people throw in praise and adoration words, when praying, that are nothing more than part of a formula - "filler" words. A person who really knows God and experiences interaction with him, though, will not be able to keep from pouring out praise from the heart.

Thanksgiving [2]

Thanksgiving simply means saying "thanks" for something that someone has done for you. You do it often when people are nice to you or when they give you something.

God has given, and continues to give, uncountable nice things to us. He gives us material objects to make our lives more comfortable. He gives us people to make our lives richer. He has even given us our very life.

But most importantly, he has given us his love and a relationship with himself. 1 Chronicles 16:34 admonishes us, "Give thanks to the LORD, for he is good; his love endures forever." We could go on for days naming the wonderful things he has given us. And if we are truly grateful, our expressions of "thanks" will flow forth without any sense of being forced.

Intercession [3]

Often our most heartfelt prayers are when we intercede for others. Samuel felt very strongly about this, even when the people he was leading were headed in the wrong direction. He told his followers, in 1 Samuel 12:23, "As for me, far be it from me that I should sin against the LORD by failing to pray for you. And I will teach you the way that is good and right."

Intercession is simply speaking up on behalf of another person. You have friends and loved ones that you want to help. If you see a situation where you can step in and make things easier for them, it makes you feel really good.

As we look around, we see where other people are struggling and we want to do something. In many of those cases, there is nothing we can do in our own strength to solve their problems. But our case is not hopeless. It is possible for us to ask God to step in and help. Our intercession to God on their behalf ought to give us the same satisfaction we would receive if we were doing something ourselves.

Petition [4]

Perhaps the most commonly used part of the prayer formula is petition. "Petition" is such a formal word, but our expression of it should not seem so formal and strange. Petition is when we put ourselves on the receiving end. It is a request in behalf of ourselves. We petition other people when we ask them for something. Every relationship has a natural give and take. We certainly give of ourselves and intercede for others, but we also make requests to have our own needs satisfied.

We should always be looking for ways to give ourselves to God, but it is also OK to ask him for things. The Bible is full of examples of petition. Just look at the Lord's Prayer. In Matthew 6:9-13, there are such phrases as, "give us today our daily bread," "forgive us our debts," "lead us not into temptation" and "deliver us from the evil one." Where we often go wrong, when we make requests, is in our attitude and mindset. We need to have the right attitude and perspective when we petition God.

So just what is that right attitude? Getting an answer to prayer is not simply about getting what we want. It is about finding out what God wants and asking for that. We have to completely put selfishness aside. Perhaps the clearest expression of this idea is found in 1 John 5:14-15 where we read, "This is the confidence we have in approaching God: that if we ask anything according to his will, he hears us. And if we know that he hears us - whatever we ask - we know that we have what we asked of him."

Again, we are back to the whole idea of relationship. Our deepest desire should be to give God everything he wants out of us, but we have to figure out what that is before we can do it. He already knows what it takes to completely fulfill our lives and is working diligently to bring it about. But the two things don't come together until we decide that we only want what God wants, and we don't want anything he doesn't want.

Perhaps one of the main reasons this is so difficult is because God sees things so differently than we see them. We get attached to earthly things and want them. God has a bigger view in mind. When we are praying for money to pay our bills, God may be wanting us to learn a lesson about faith. We may have to struggle a little before we see the answer that is really the best one. When we pray that someone will get well, or not die, we often have a selfish motive and are not aware of what God is trying to do with that person or with ourself.

But when we can give ourselves to God completely and learn to see things through his eyes, we will begin to see the larger purpose in what is going on around us. We will also begin learning to pray according to the will of God. Then we will see answers like we have never seen before.

Confession [5]

Every relationship has those moments when someone does something that causes offense to the other. When that happens, the relationship is strained. The only way to get the problem out in the open, so that it can be taken care of, is to confess the wrong. Confession is simply admitting that we have done something wrong.

When we offend God (when we sin), we strain the relationship with him. As long as we hold onto that wrong, the strain can't be relieved. God has given us very specific instructions about how to take care of these kinds of problems. In 1 John 1:9, we read, "If we confess our sins, he is faithful and just and will forgive us our sins and purify us from all unrighteousness." When we create distance between ourselves and God, at some point we have to confess it to him so we can get the conversation going again.

Repentance [6]

Repentance is nothing more than saying you are sorry and really meaning it, to the point you make a change. When we offend or hurt someone, the offense is on our own shoulders, and we are responsible for doing something to make up for it. We have to confess our wrongdoing to get the conversation going again, but that is not enough. We have to take the next step to own up to our responsibility and change our attitude and behavior. That is repentance.

God never does anything that requires him to confess and repent to us, but we do things against him that make it necessary for us to change our hearts. When we offend God and mess up the relationship, we have to admit it to ourselves and to him, then take steps to right the wrong. He has made it clear that this is a necessity. In Hosea 14:1, we read these words, "Return, O Israel, to the LORD your God. Your sins have been your downfall!" We return to God by sincerely giving up the wrong and turning away from its root cause.

Asking God Questions [7]

Up until now we have focused on the elements of prayer that are most commonly recognized and talked about. Beginning with this topic we move beyond the "formula" that is generally associated with prayer and will look at other aspects of praying that are found in scripture.

In the course of normal conversation we think of things that we don't know, but which our partner does, so we ask questions. What could be more natural than that? We ask questions about how the other person is doing, about what they are doing and even about things that we don't know but want to understand.

There are certainly many things about life and eternity that we don't know, and the only source of information about these areas is God himself. So, it is natural that we ask him questions about these things. The prophet Jeremiah asked God why the wicked seem to prosper. Job asked God why he was going through so much affliction when he had been such a good person. When we ask God questions, he will eventually reveal new things to us. The answers may be different from what we expect, but the process of asking questions is an important part of the conversation.

Questioning God [8]

Every relationship has its difficult moments. Bad things happen and sometimes we think it is our partner's fault. When we think that way, we naturally question the other person. Now this doesn't mean it really was their fault, but until we can sort it out we may go through a questioning process.

Certainly God never does anything to cause us harm. But sometimes, when bad things happen that are beyond our understanding or control, we wonder why God allowed that in our life. As long as we maintain the right attitude, it is quite alright to question God. In Job chapter seven, we see another example of it from Job's life. Abraham questioned God in Genesis 15 concerning how he was going to pass on his lineage. Questioning God is OK. We just have to be sure that when we do, we keep in mind that he is the almighty and all-knowing one and that the progress of history moves according to his purposes, not our own.

Making Promises [9]

Another important aspect of a relationship relates to the effort to strengthen it. One of the very effective relationship strengthening devices is a promise. There is a promise in a wedding ceremony. People also make promises to each other to stay in touch or to keep a friendship alive. In fact, even if it is never spoken, there is an implied promise to stay close in every relationship that exists.

When we enter into a relationship with God, we are entering into a covenant - a type of promise. Then, as we live within that covenant, we recognize more and more the nature of the relationship and try to strengthen it.

People sometimes make other kinds of promises to God, and these promises come in many forms. Some people tell God that, "If you will___, then I will___." David did this in Psalm 51:12-13 when he said, "Restore to me the joy of your salvation and grant me a willing spirit, to sustain me. Then I will teach transgressors your ways, and sinners will turn back to you." Sometimes people just want to be closer to God, so they promise to follow him no matter what. David did it in Psalm 86:7, when he said, "In the day of my trouble I will call to you, for you will answer me." Regardless of the particular form, promises are an avenue of communication that clearly fit into the prayer process.

Submission to God [10]

Many people have the sense that submitting to someone means giving away their free will. That is only the case in situations where someone is bullying you and you give in to them under threat of force. But in a loving relationship submission is voluntary - it is the desired state.

Submission is not simply a matter of giving in to what the other person wants. Rather, it is the giving of yourself to the other person. No healthy relationship can exist without this being an integral part of it. Then, when you are in that state of submission, you are not looking for ways to assert your independence. Rather, you are looking for ways to please the other person and make the bond stronger.

A relationship with God is no different. A lot of people chafe at submitting to God because they don't want to comply with what they consider stringent moral demands. But this discomfort only goes to prove that there is no relationship with him in the first place. When the love is there, the desire to please is very strong. And when the desire to please is that strong, it is no big deal to submit to the things that make it possible to have a deeper relationship with him.

In Ephesians 5:21, we read some very profound words. It says, "Submit to one another out of reverence for Christ." When understood correctly, this kind of submission becomes one of the most powerful magnets in existence for pulling individuals into a relationship.

Worshiping [11]

To worship is to venerate, or to honor and love with deep devotion. People express this in many ways. Some express this kind of devotion to inanimate objects, like money. It may also be expressed toward people who are very highly respected. In human relationships where the level of love and respect are high, honor is not an unusual byproduct.

The place where this kind of veneration is most expected, however, is in our relationship with God. Because of the fact that he is Lord of all, God is worthy of every bit of devotion and respect we can muster.

In Isaiah 6:1-8, we find two of the most profound expressions of worship imaginable. The first is the worship of the angels themselves as they say, "Holy, holy, holy is the LORD Almighty; the whole earth is full of his glory." Then, as Isaiah finds himself in the presence of the Lord, he can't help but bow down in his presence and say, "My eyes have seen the King, the LORD Almighty." This should be the experience of every one of us. Expressing this kind of respect to God is a wonderful utterance which will flow naturally as we actually step into his presence.

Random Conversation [12]

Not all interaction with another person is full of deep significance. There are routine parts of our lives that actually make up the bulk of our living. People in a relationship also share these routine times. It is not unusual, at all, for me and my wife to talk about the yard or the weather or what happened at work, and so on. While these things are certainly mundane, they are not unimportant. This routine conversation keeps us connected with each other at the most basic level.

We ought to be able to relate with God at this level, too. He is vitally interested in every aspect of our lives. And while he knows all of the routine things about our lives without us having to tell him, that is not the point - he knows the profound things about us, too. We need to engage him on this level regardless of the importance of the topic.

The Bible is full of examples of people relating to God in this manner. Almost the whole of Psalm 31 reflects David talking to God about the routine matters of life. He talks about such things as his disdain for idols, his personal pain and his struggle with people who don't like him. We see Jesus doing the same thing in the seventeenth chapter of John where he talks about such things as the relationship he and God have, about his interaction with his disciples and how people in the world treat and think of him. Relationship requires interaction, and we cannot enhance our relationship with God unless we take the time to talk with him. This includes the routine aspects of life.

Rebellion from God [13]

There is a type of conversation that destroys rather than strengthens a relationship. It happens when a person deliberately speaks to another with the intention of breaking a relationship off or preventing it from ever happening. We see this in instances where someone feels betrayed, or has found a "new love," or simply wants to go in a different direction in life.

Typically, we don't consider this type of conversation to be a positive thing, and we certainly don't think of it as an element that should be a part of praying. But the process of communicating with God is, by definition, prayer - even if it is a rejection of him. There are actually cases of this happening in the Bible. In Daniel chapter 9, Daniel prayed and expressed Israel's rejection of God. In verse 11 we read these words, "All Israel has transgressed your law and turned away, refusing to obey you."

Now this is not something that should ever be a part of the interaction of an individual and God. It is simply included here because there are instances in the Bible where this kind of communication takes place and I wanted to lay out the full range of prayer possibilities.

Answers from God [14]

All of the prayer categories to this point express the idea that the essence of prayer is communication with God. It is not a formula or ritual that a person goes through in order to manipulate life.

In addition, the categories above relate primarily to one way communication - from us to God. But real communication must be two way. There certainly must be parts of the conversation where God speaks back. And, in fact, this is the case. The following four areas focus on communication that comes the other way - from God to us.

In a conversation, when one person asks a question, the other person typically gives some kind of answer. The question may be related to something routine or something profound, something about the other person's life or something that we want to know from them.

As we saw above, asking questions of God is a natural and normal part of any conversation with him. And when we ask him questions, he most assuredly answers them. It will most likely not be in an audible voice, but he will answer. The answers typically come in one of several forms.

Sometimes the answers emerge from our circumstances. Often, when we ask God questions, he puts us in a situation which is, itself, the answer. God answered Elijah this way when he confronted the prophets of Baal in 1 Kings chapter eighteen. When Elijah prayed for God to reveal himself, and God sent down fire from heaven, the resulting circumstance left no doubt as to which God was the real one.

Another way God answers is from his revelation. Many of the answers to the questions we ask God are already written in the Bible. As we read and study it, we come across the answers that we seek. We all have issues and struggles in life and end up asking God questions for which there are already answers. There are answers to such questions as, "How can I endure my current trial?," or "How should I react toward the person who is aggravating me?," and a whole host of other issues.

The other typical way God replies to us is as he directly impresses the answer on our hearts as we connect with him spirit to spirit. We see an example of how God's spirit answered Paul's question about where to minister when God sent him to Macedonia in the sixteenth chapter of Acts.

God has numerous ways of communicating to us. We only have to learn to be attentive, have a searching heart and be open to his communications, in order to receive the answers.

Calling from God [15]

In any interaction, your relationship partner will have things they want you to do. It is the reciprocal part of your having things you want from them. If it is a really significant relationship, we will to try and accommodate those desires to the highest degree possible.

God has things that he wants us to do, too - only his desires take us to an entirely different level. God has a vested interest in having us develop to the highest level possible. He created us to fulfill a particular mission in life. We will never find personal fulfillment unless we understand and pursue that mission. The way he lets us know about it is by means of a calling. In Acts chapter nine we see two distinct examples of this in action. The first one is long term, and the second one was a calling to do a single project.

First, we see God calling Paul to become a missionary to the non-Jewish world of his day. This, for Paul, represented a career change. He had to change from being a Jewish religious leader to a Christian missionary.

The second type of calling we see is like the one God gave to Ananias when he told him to go see Paul and free him from his blindness. Even though this was a one time event, Ananias considered it very risky because of the fact that Paul had come to his city in order to kill and imprison people like him. In both cases, the individuals had to choose whether or not they would positively respond to God's calling. In both of these cases, they responded positively and God blessed them.

God is constantly and actively engaged in communicating to us the specific calling that will allow us to fulfill the mission he has for us. It is up to us to tune into his communication and to respond when we hear him.

Instruction from God [16]

Every one of us has things that we are good at and things we are not good at - things we know and things we don't know. But even what we know is not complete. It is always possible for us to grow beyond where we already are. One of the primary ways we acquire that higher level of knowledge is to allow someone we trust and respect to teach us.

There are many things that are not possible for us to know by natural means - particularly that which relates to spiritual reality. We would not know how to invite Christ into our lives if God had not revealed it to us in his revelation. There are many other things, as well, that we learn about God and his purposes from the Bible. Other things he reveals to us directly, as he sometimes does in answering our questions or in giving us our calling.

Judgment from God [17]

When we do things to offend another person, there is typically some kind of consequence. It may or may not be a direct action from the offended person, but the consequence happens just the same. Sometimes that aftermath is a guilty conscience or a feeling of regret. Sometime, though, the offended individual does do something directly to make us feel a result from the action.

When we offend God, there is also some kind of consequence. The word "judgment" usually makes us think of something very stringent and horrible, but all we are really talking about, here, is the direct result of bad thoughts and actions. Sometimes judgments on us are severe and even life-threatening or life-taking. God gave this kind of judgment to Sodom and Gomorrah in order to punish them for their horrible sins. Other times, judgment is simply God allowing us to reap the natural consequences of our actions. This may be as severe as a person going to jail for a crime, or as inward as an individual's inner guilt or regret.

When judgment is appropriate, God always lets us know. But his purpose is never to just punish us. He wants us to understand the problem, learn from it and repent, so we can keep the relationship strong.

The Reason

The reason for this chapter is simply to make the point, loud and clear, that prayer is not simply a formula, it is a conversation - a real conversation. It is the communication that takes place between an individual and God. It is more than the five elements that are typically associated with praying. It is more than an empty shell. It covers every possible aspect and method of communicating. Only when we understand what praying really is, are we able to begin the journey of making it a reality in our own lives.

Digging Deeper

- Think about a typical time when you engage in prayer. Do you only do it at formal times like the blessing before meal or at a gathering of Christians?

- When you spend time in private prayer, do you ever get outside of "the formula?" In your private prayer times, what is the evidence that you are truly connecting heart to heart with God?

- How effective are your spiritual listening skills? What are some things that God has told you lately in your conversations with him?

- Go back through the categories of praying above and try to think of some things in each one that you have conversed with God about. What are some things that you would like to talk to him about that you have not? What can you do to hear his communications more clearly?

I have already mentioned the struggle I have had between interacting with God based on knowledge vs. experience. We have to have a knowledge base in order to know how to approach an interaction with God. But the act of praying is experiential - it is the actual connection we have with God.

I have been able to identify elements of that experience and describe them, to a degree. But I am not able to give the experience to someone else. I can only point the way. For me, it is a frustration to hold within my own experience something so powerful and profound and not be able to actually give it to someone.

I experience the same thing, sometimes, when I teach karate. It is possible to point someone to a higher level of growth, but they will never know it until they actually work themselves up to the level where they can experience it for themselves.

Higher and higher levels of intimacy with God are there for the taking. Anyone can experience it. You can experience it. But it will not happen until you take yourself on the journey.

Chapter 5
How to Get Close to God

Getting close to God

Think of a person that you have a very close relationship with - a spouse, fiancé, parent, child, grandparent. . . , just whoever. How would you characterize that relationship? Are you satisfied just to think about them? Sure, if you are not able to be with them in person it is a joy to think about how wonderful they are to you. But is that ultimately good enough? Would you be satisfied just to think and think about them, but never be able to spend time together? How crazy is that?

When I was living in Eastern Europe, I accepted a project that required me to spend three weeks in Germany. Now make no mistake, it was not a bad assignment. I got to go all over the country, see a lot of interesting places and meet a lot of great people. But, there was a huge drawback. I had to go alone and leave my wife and son behind. I love both of them more than words can say and, in spite of the good time I had doing the project, I really missed my family. They are the ones on earth that I love more than anyone or anything else.

In order for a relationship to achieve its ultimate potential, there has to be actual personal interaction. If there is not shared experience, a relationship cannot grow deeper. In fact, it is just the opposite. Contrary to the popular expression that absence makes the heart grow fonder, in truth, absence causes estrangement.

We have an actual need for relationship, and we will seek it out with those we have access to. If someone we deeply care for moves out of our life, we will not forget them, but we will move on to other relationships.

This is one of the huge reasons why many people never feel close to God - they don't spend any personal time with him. It is like they live in a different city and only call him up once in a while to say hello. To be close we have to stay close.

Since God is personal, our interaction with him comes in the form of a relationship. These interactions with him are not mere intellectual exercises, they are actual real experiences. We have to live them out in life. We have to learn how to make our interaction with God as close, personal and meaningful as the interaction we have with the person on earth that we love the most. If you do not know a relationship with God as a real objective experience, you have missed the most dynamic part of knowing God.

A relationship with God is not a subjective feeling, though feelings will certainly come into play at various times. It is real interaction with a real person. Whether you feel it or not is beside the point. We feel a lot of things. If, for some reason, a relationship experience is bad, our tendency is to conclude that there is something wrong with relationships in general. We may think that if a relationship goes sour it is because the relationship itself is wrong. That is absolutely not true! Relationships are inherently good. But many people simply do not have good relationship skills. When that is the case, the proper response is not to run from the relationship, but to hone your relationship skills so that you can become good at it.

Each relationship is going to be a little different because the personalities involved are different. You can't relate the same way to an "intellectual" as you do with a "touchy-feely" person. You have to adjust your interaction based on the characteristics of the other person.

This principle is absolutely critical when thinking about a relationship with God. He is a unique personality, and we have to relate to him based on who he is.

We have already looked at who God is, as regards his personhood. But there is another aspect of his being that we also have to know - his personality. Think about it. You know people that you like and people that you don't like. Why is that so? Well, you tend to like those who have interests and personality traits that compliment yours. And you tend not to like people who's personality and interests are not complimentary.

Looking at it this way, it is easy to see why we might be attracted (or not attracted) to God. If you exhibit life characteristics that are similar to his, you will feel comfortable with him. If you live by a different set of values, you will find that you are not very comfortable with him.

So just what is God's personality like? He is:

- Love [1] - If you don't have a loving heart you are not going to feel comfortable with God.
- Holy [2] - If you allow a lot of impure thoughts and deeds into your life, you are not going to find God very appealing.
- Merciful [3] - If you are not a forgiving person, you will find being in God's presence uncomfortable.
- Giving [4] - If you are self-centered and stingy, you will feel uncomfortable in God's presence.
- Good [5] - Everyone has some good in them, but if you are one who enjoys creating mischief or doing bad things to other people, you will not want to spend much time with God.
- Righteous [6] - If you are one who gets upset with God when he punishes those who do wrong, or when he tries

to discipline wrongdoing, you are not going to like God very much.
- Patient [7] - If you are not willing to relax and allow things to work out in God's timing, you are going to quickly get frustrated with God.

We could go on, but I think you get the point. God has a particular personality, and we either like being around the kind of person he is, or we don't.

So here is the bottom line. God is not going to change! His personality is the baseline standard for those who want to spend eternity in heaven. His personality is right. If we have a problem with that, God is not the one that needs to change, we are.

I know people who simply do not want to change, even for God. They have a lifestyle that goes against God's ways, or have a worldview that relegates God to the sideline, and have decided they are not going to change no matter what. For the person who has chosen to take that course, there is not much that can be done to help their praying. They will be uncomfortable in God's presence and not pursue the relationship. If you find yourself feeling uncomfortable with God, you might want to examine how your life stacks up to him, and you may just find the problem.

For those, though, who want to get closer to God, there are some things that can be done to make it happen. Let's explore how we can interact with God in the most exciting and powerful relationship that is possible to experience.

The Attitude

This section on attitude may be the most important thing written in this entire book. If there is anything that separates the wimps from the non-wimps when it comes to praying, this is it. Our attitudes determine the way we interact in any arena, whether it is with a wall or with a human being. If our attitude is happy, we will interact one way. If we are angry, we will interact another way. There are literally dozens of different attitude postures we can take, and each one causes us to relate in a different way.

When it comes to relationships, this concept is decisive. If you feel superior to another person, you will relate to them as if they are less than you. If you feel insecure, you will relate to them out of fear or timidity. This principle is certainly true as we relate to other people, and we can readily see how it works out in daily life.

One day, while I was living in Latvia, I was downtown and saw a woman walking toward me. She was dressed kind of "ratty" but otherwise seemed fine. All of a sudden she stopped on the corner, slumped down in the middle of the sidewalk and took on one of the most pitiful looking postures I have ever seen. She then held out her hand and began to beg. In that position she looked like a poor, crippled, helpless soul. The transformation was nothing short of amazing. But it was all a ploy to get sympathy and money. That event had a profound impact on the way I viewed the street beggars from that day on. I certainly would not have given her any money, and became quite careful any time I considered giving money to anyone who was begging.

When it comes to our relationship with God, the same principle of attitude holds true. We will interact based on our attitude toward him. If we want to have a wonderful relationship with him, we have to interact with him with the right kind of attitude.

So what should be our posture before God? We need to recognize that he is the one who is the Lord, and that we have to accommodate him - not vice versa. We are the ones who are frail and full of sin. From an outside perspective it doesn't seem that God and mankind would even be a likely relationship match. You have probably heard the expressions, or used them yourself, that we humans are "worms" or the "dust of the earth" or "filthy rags." Certainly compared to God that is exactly what we are. But he doesn't see us that way. He sees us as individuals whom he loves and who have tremendous potential for growth - and he tries to relate to us on that basis.

But God can't live our lives for us. We are responsible for creating our own perspective that allows the relationship to go forward. When we begin praying with God, we have to recognize that we are able to have that kind of interaction because he has provided a way for us to have our weakness and impurity set aside. We need to take full advantage of the privilege to personally interact with him, but we must still have the humility to acknowledge his majesty and holiness. He is, after all, God!

Our first act in prayer, every time we consciously come into his presence, should be to express his worthiness. We should have him on a pedestal. We should recognize what a privilege and honor it is to be able to have a personal relationship with the God who created the universe. We should recognize his might and majesty. This does not mean we need to be cowering in fear. He really does love us and has our best interest at heart at every moment. His purpose is to build us up to the highest degree possible. But we ought never take that for granted. Our attitude toward him should always be the most profound love, the highest respect and deepest humility. We need to feel it in our hearts and express it with our words.

One of the best demonstrations of this attitude, in the Bible, was at one of the deepest spiritual struggles that Jesus ever faced. Just before his crucifixion, as he was praying in the Garden of Gethsemane, he was trying to come to a personal resolution, with God, regarding his very life. He knew that the reason he was even on earth was to die as a sacrifice for the sins of mankind. He had geared his whole life to accomplish that task. But as the moment approached, he knew the agony he was in for and, as a human, didn't want to go through it. So he begged God to let him off the hook. But in that moment of passion he did not lose his perspective. His attitude was that, ultimately, he was committed to carrying out God's will, no matter what! He prayed with the deepest sincerity, "Not my will but yours."[8] He recognized that God was the king, not himself. He humbled himself before the will of God, no matter the outcome.

Let's look at one other scripture that takes us to the very heart of this matter. In Luke 9:23-25, Jesus was teaching and he made this statement, "If anyone would come after me, he must deny himself and take up his cross daily and follow me. For whoever wants to save his life will lose it, but whoever loses his life for me will save it."

What is Jesus saying here? He is telling those who want to be in relationship with him, that they must acknowledge him as the owner of their lives. "Denying self" means that an individual must be looking outside of self for direction in every aspect of life. "Taking up your cross" means setting yourself up for execution. "Follow me" means to hand over control of the direction of your life to Christ. Put all of this together and it means you are willing, at every moment, to lay aside any and every part of your existence to follow the will of God.

Think about it this way. If you had a clear word from God right now, would you be willing to quit your job, sell your house, give away all your money, and leave your hometown to go back to school so you could train to become a missionary to Bangladesh?

You think that is tough, how about this one? If you had a clear communication from God, would you sign all of your personal possessions over to another person and just walk away? Would you be willing to release your child or spouse into the hands of God and permit him to take them in any direction he wanted to - including to their death, if that fit his purposes?

Do I have your attention yet? This attitude that we must take on means that we, literally, acknowledge God as the king of our life, and submit to his will in everything. Understand this! In most cases God is not going to ask you to give up all your money, change jobs, move to Bangladesh or ask for the life of someone you love. Mostly he has put you in the place you are so that he can work though your life where you are. But he does have special missions for some people which requires an unusual kind of sacrifice. And if you happen to be one of those, you have to be willing to let it happen, even if it does mean giving up what you already know and have.

When I pray, the first thing I do is acknowledge God as my king. I offer him my job, my hobbies, my family, even my very life. I give them to him to use as he desires. In my heart of hearts I don't want him to ask me to move, take my wife or allow me to get cancer. But if that is what he needs from me in order to accomplish his purposes through my life, it is on the table.

When we go before God the first thing we must do is recognize him as the king. We must lay our heart and soul before him as an offering. When we enter his presence with the right attitude, we have put ourselves into a position to profoundly experience a relationship with him. At that point we have come to God on his terms, which opens up the door to a deep and profound interaction with him.

The Touch

I remember way back when I was a teenager and first started getting interested in girls. It was kind of an awkward time. During that era of my life there were some girls that I thought were pretty and wanted to get to know a little better. As it turned out, there were some who wanted to get to know me better, too. But, at that age, there was a little ritual that had to play out where we first talked and flirted for a while.

I remember one time in particular when I took a girl to the movies. We sat there for a while side by side, then, when I was pretty confident that I would not be rejected, I reached out to hold her hand. The moment she responded back positively, I was on cloud nine. A simple touch was a powerful and exciting event in getting that relationship going.

When dealing with God, once we have brought ourselves to the right attitude, we must open ourselves up to his presence. The tendency of many people is to keep God at arms length, out of awe or fear or even discomfort. In spite of the fact that God could act superior and relate to us as a dominating and fearsome taskmaster, he has presented himself to us differently. He loves us and wants to spend time with us. He has revealed himself to us as a father and friend. The next step in praying is to acknowledge the relationship.

It is not presumption on our part to enter directly into his presence. He is the one who decided that it should be that way. He is the one who made it possible for personal interaction to happen. He is the one who actually takes the initiative in the process.

So, instead of trying to keep God at a distance, it is important to allow him to actually come to you and to be personal. This cannot happen if you have not already taken on the right attitude but, if you have, you can actually step into the very presence of God.

Imagine him walking up to you, stopping right in front of your face, then reaching out and putting his hand on your shoulder. Feel the touch of his hand. Instead of tensing up, relax and allow yourself to be comfortable in his presence. This may actually take some work for those who are not used to being personal with God. But by it, you not only acknowledge his initiative on your behalf, you actually open yourself to a personal relationship with him.

The Embrace

I love my wife deeply, and sometimes when we are together, even in a room full of people, we will hold hands or touch each other affectionately. It is a way for us to tangibly express our connection with each other. But when we really want to express our love at a deep level, we go beyond a simple touch. We embrace and give ourselves to each other body and soul.

A spiritual embrace with God takes us deeper into personal interaction with him. Praying is not real until you are in his presence and interacting with him at the most personal level. It is more than just talking, you have to actually experience him with you. Again, this experience is not limited to feelings, and it goes beyond the speaking of words. While feelings may be involved at particular times, the primary issue is personal consciousness.

The mechanism that allows this to happen is our imagination. This does not mean that the interaction is not real. It is very real. Our imagination simply allows us to conceive of its operation. This is the place where we allow God to envelop us in his love. When we have come to the place where we are sure of his existence and presence with us, we become conscious of the spiritual connection we have with him. It is the *being* part of relationship, as opposed to the *doing*.

When God steps into our presence and reaches down to touch us (as was mentioned above), that is his gesture to let us know that we are accepted by him. At that point it is appropriate to express our love back to him. We can do this by imagining an embrace with him. Even though we do this by an act of our imagination, we have to understand that the embrace is real - even if not physical. And no matter how we experience it emotionally or mentally, this interaction with God is an expression of an actual personal relationship with him.

When we take the step to imagine that we are actually engaged in an embrace with God, it is quite possible to have a sense of his presence and to be overcome with emotion. Those kinds of feelings are a wonderful experience and something to be treasured. But feeling is not a necessary part of the process. Remember, God is not a feeling, he is a real, objective person, and our relationship with him is not validated by feeling. Relationship either exists or not based on whether it has ever been established.

Feelings are affected by a lot of things. They can be affected by how well we slept the night before, what we ate for lunch, what someone said to us or even the phase of the moon. Good feelings are a treasure, but they are not a measure of our relationship with God. The relationship is an objective reality no matter how we feel.

The Communication

The deepest and most profound earthly relationship I have is with my wife, but she is not the only one that I have a close relationship with. Flinn is a friend of mine who lives in Georgia. We met in graduate school and from that time on our families have been close.

There have been times over the years, in my life and his, when we have gone through some very tough struggles. We developed what we called a "pity party." We would just get together, fix some popcorn, drink some lemonade and talk. And you know what? The communication helped us get through the struggles. Sometimes it was the advice. Sometimes it was just the company. But interacting at a deep spiritual level with him has made a difference in my life.

Up until this point, we have focused on making ourselves conscious of the connection we have with God. This is important because it gets us prepared to interact in a powerful and intentional way. But the connection is only the starting point. After experiencing the connection we must then begin to engage him in conversation. This conversation should touch on all of the topics that we would talk about with any other person.

Think back to the discussion in chapter four. There are all kinds of things we talk about with other individuals as we engage in conversation. These same things, along with a couple of special ones, are also topics that we should take up with God. As you will recall, those topics included:

- Praise and Adoration
- Thanksgiving
- Intercession
- Petition
- Confession
- Repentance
- Asking God Questions
- Questioning God
- Making Promises
- Submission to God
- Worshiping
- Random Conversation
- Receiving Answers
- Receiving a Calling
- Receiving Instruction

We have to remember that, even though we use many of the same categories for prayer that we use in human conversation, we experience the process differently. In human interaction we have a physical person that we can feel, see and audibly hear. When interacting with God, it is a purely spiritual interaction and we have to learn to operate in that arena.

Since we are spiritual beings, and our spiritual part encompasses all of the self-conscious and decision making capabilities that we have, we use those capabilities when communicating with God. That is what is involved in the various aspects of praying that have been mentioned above. But there is another part of communicating with God that we need to mention, as well. Since spiritual reality is so far beyond our ability to comprehend, and God is so far beyond our full knowledge, there are communications that we want, and need, to express to him that we really don't know how to do.

God has that covered, as well. He has provided a purely spiritual communication medium where his spirit connects directly with our spirit. He reads and interprets the deep thoughts and desires of our being in a way that corresponds with the way spiritual reality works. In Romans 8:26-27, we read about this. It says, "In the same way, the Spirit helps us in our weakness. We do not know what we ought to pray for, but the Spirit himself intercedes for us with groans that words cannot express. And he who searches our hearts knows the mind of the Spirit, because the Spirit intercedes for the saints in accordance with God's will." To interact this way requires that we learn and practice the spiritual disciplines that get us connected with God, and do it at a level beyond anything we can ever experience with another human being.

While our interaction with God is purely spiritual, we still have to work at it from within the physical arena. We have to engage our body, our minds and our feelings, as well as our spirit (we will get into the physical part more in the next chapter). But the important point to grasp, at this moment, is that we are able to have an intentional, conscious and objective conversation with a real person who wants to communicate with us.

The Ongoing Fellowship

I have already mentioned my relationship with my wife. It is as profound a relationship as I can imagine in the physical world. I treasure the time we are together. But there are times when we are not together. One of us runs errands, goes to work, goes to visit family or friends, or even just gets involved in some activity at home where the entire focus is elsewhere. Does the relationship end when we are not in physical proximity, or when we are thinking about other things? Absolutely not! And our relationship with God has this element to it, as well.

Many people think about prayer as those moments when we actually take time out to consciously engage God in conversation. Certainly that is an important, even vital, part of the equation. But just as the relationship between two physical individuals does not end when we are apart, our relationship with God does not end when we begin engaging in life's routine activities.

When we leave the immediate interaction of a prayer opportunity, or "quiet time," we have to realize that we have not really left God's presence. The prayer opportunity is simply the time when we put all of our focus on experiencing his presence with us. When we leave that, we have not left him. He is still walking with us throughout the other parts of our lives, even when our concentration is in other places.

It is not enough to pop in and out of the presence of God. We have to give ourselves to him so that we live all of life in his presence. Not that we are always thinking about him, but we live our lives " as if " we were. To do that we have to create good spiritual habits.

Experiencing Praying

Prayer is not a feeling. Praying is not simply a time when we tell God what we want. It is personal interaction with a personal God who has revealed himself to us as father and friend. We experience prayer when we interact with him on this personal level - in the give and take of a special spiritual conversation.

The experience of praying is felt in the context of our physical reality, but the praying itself takes place in a different arena - the arena of the spirit. When we engage God, it is as one spirit to another, and the communication that happens transcends the physical world we live in.

About now you should begin to get the sense that praying is more than just taking a few moments to utter a few words. It is a profound interaction that requires our attention and effort. A person who doesn't want to put this kind of effort into the relationship will never experience the fullness of a relationship with God.

We cannot depend on feelings to define our praying. Our conversation with God is an objective reality no matter how we feel. Praying is, certainly, not for wimps!

Digging Deeper

- How would you characterize your current relationship with God? What would you *not* be willing to give up for him?

- When you think about getting close to God, what do you imagine? Can you see yourself touching and embracing him?

- When you are really ready to get serious about your relationship with God, set aside some time and start giving him the various pieces of your life. Give him your job, your material possessions, your family members, etc. Acknowledge him as your sovereign, and open yourself to go anywhere, or do anything, he asks.

In some ways it is difficult to talk about my experience with God. I experience his touch, and sometimes I feel emotion along with it, but it is not a physical experience. There may be physical effects, but the experience itself is spiritual.

There is a part of my being that reaches out beyond the limitations of my physical existence. I experience it but can't fully describe it. When I have myself in a position to interact with God, I actually experience his presence (I really don't want to use the word feel). He is there with me.

When I interact with God he communicates with me. It is not like I hear audible voices, or anything like that. But when I read and meditate on Scripture, I discern deeper truth that I did not have before. When I ask him to help me understand the right thing to do, he somehow reveals that to my spirit.

Learning to operate on that level, though, has been a process of growth - and I am still growing. I have had to put myself in a position where I was able to discern the spiritual arena. I have had to learn to hear God's "voice" and prompting. I don't understand it, but it exists. It is operative in my life. And, I believe that this level of communication can operate in anyone's life who makes the effort to develop it.

Chapter 6
The Place Where the Body Touches the Spirit

I remember a number of years ago, I decided I needed to get in shape. I had been neglecting regular exercise for some time and had physically gotten to a place I didn't want to be. So, I decided that I would begin running. The next morning I got up, got dressed and hit the street - and what a horrible experience that was! I was so out of shape. I ran a short distance then had to stop and walk a while. Then I would run a little more and have to stop again. Let's just say that I didn't set any land speed records that day. When I got home, I nearly died.

In spite of all the agony, I kept at it every day. And after about a month my persistence began to pay off. Whereas in the beginning I was barely able to make it around the block, after my conditioning began to kick in, I was going as much as five or six miles without stopping.

Just because my body was capable of being in condition didn't mean that it automatically would be. In order to reach that goal I had to put out effort. And not just any effort would do. It had to be effort directed specifically at what I wanted to accomplish.

As spiritual beings we have the ability to relate personally with God. But just because we have that capability doesn't mean that we automatically do it. This also takes effort. We literally have to train ourselves to operate in that arena.

But there is more to it than that. As physical beings we have to train ourselves to operate on a spiritual level from the platform of a physical body. This kind of training requires effort in every part of our being - with the emotions, the body and the brain.

Living life in the presence of God is an objective reality. God is there whether we admit it or not. He is there whether we feel it or not. He is there even if we don't want him to be, though hopefully, it is everyone's intention to experience his presence. And while it is not necessary for us to feel it in order for him to be there, it is a wonderful affirmation when we do.

But the unfortunate situation is, we all tend to base a lot of our experience with God on our feelings. The tendency is to think that when we don't feel him he is not there, and when we do feel him he is. Intellectually we may acknowledge that this is not true, but most people live their lives as if it were true, anyhow.

As was noted earlier, our feelings are physical sensations that are affected by a lot of things. But while there are a lot of things that affect our emotions, human beings have a unique ability to operate from the other side, as well - to affect and control our emotions by deliberate decisions. We can actually manipulate how we feel. The feeling may or may not have anything to do with our actual situation. We can, for instance, train ourselves to feel good in a horrible situation. The apostle Paul sang songs while he was in prison after having been beaten. We can train ourselves to have good feelings when we are fatigued. So why not train ourselves to feel the presence of God when we are praying?

This is actually not as far fetched as you might think. Even though how we feel does not affect whether or not God is really present with us, if we can learn to control our feelings that way, it can make it much easier to experience God in our lives on an ongoing basis.

What we are talking about is learning to control the physical portions of our lives. This includes our emotions, our body and our brain function. Let's look at those three areas and see what we can do to give ourselves an edge.

Physical Control Part I - The Feelings

It has already been mentioned that there are a lot of things that affect how we feel. By the same token, there are a lot of actions that we can take to change how we feel at any given moment. The trick is to recognize when negative emotions are ruling, know what to do when we recognize it, then to do something about it.

Recognizing Negative Emotions

I remember one very dark period in my life. It was dark because I was emotionally wrung out. I experienced burnout with my work and it affected every part of my life. The hardest thing I remember dealing with was a smoldering anger that began to bubble up within me. It got to the point that I would blow up at just about anything. What made it even worse was that I recognized what was happening and hated it, but couldn't seem to do anything about it.

I finally came to a place where I was able to get the pressure off by getting out of the situation that was stressing me so highly. But then I noticed something else. I had stored that anger for such a long period of time, that even though I was no longer in the stressful situation, I still had that inner cauldron boiling up inside me. My anger had, literally, become a habit.

One day, I finally decided I was going to figure out how to deal with it once and for all. I learned to notice the emotional point where anger started in me, then developed some techniques to stop it before it erupted. It actually took two or three months of deliberate effort on my part to master it. But I did! I was able to make that change and it has had a profound impact on my life from that day on.

There is nothing strange or unusual about realizing when we are not in control of negative emotions. One of the powerful and unique aspects of humanity is that we can become aware of what is going on inside of us. Not only that, once we recognize it, we have the ability to take control and change how we feel. There is no magic formula to this. It is simply a matter of determining what negative emotions you want to recognize, then placing that in your awareness as often as possible. Over time you will be able to perceive it instantly.

What to Do When You Recognize It
There are a lot of things that we can do to change how we feel at any given moment. The possibilities below are not an exhaustive list, but they do demonstrate some of the possibilities.

Physical Exertion
One way to change how you feel is to exert positive energy. What I mean by this is to physically do something that causes you to feel good. For instance, if you jump up and down and start screaming "Yipeeee! Yipeeee!," it will make you feel better. This activity does some things to cause changes in your body. It bumps up your blood pressure and your blood temperature, it causes your body to release adrenalin, it gets your heart rate up, it gets more oxygen into your system, it increases blood circulation and it causes your brain to release endorphins. All of this together physically makes you feel better. You can create a lot of the same changes by simply getting out there and swimming, walking or almost any other kind of physical exercise.

Most people don't want to do these kinds of things when they feel emotionally down. Why? Because they don't *feel* like it. But that is precisely the point. Getting your body going may be a struggle when you feel down, but exertion will turn it around. We have the ability to override our feelings and make ourselves feel better by physical exertion.

Association vs. Disassociation

Another key to controlling our feelings relates to how we mentally associate into a situation. We experience things either subjectively or objectively. Subjective experience associates us into our feelings and makes, or allows, us to feel them. Objective experience removes us a step from our feelings so that we don't feel emotion so strongly.

When we associate with something, we experience it as involving us personally. When we understand something to be connected to us personally, we "feel" it and can experience it as good or bad. If we experience it as good, we feel good. If we experience it as bad, we feel bad.

Disassociation is when we look at something objectively. There are things that happen around us that we don't take personally. We look at them as an objective observer and study them. In that case we don't "feel" anything in particular - we just observe.

Even though we experience both association and disassociation in our lives, in most cases we don't choose when we will feel them one way or the other. Usually it just happens based on our previous experiences.

But it doesn't have to be involuntary. We have the ability to intentionally decide to associate into, or disassociate out of, an emotion. Once we recognize that we are experiencing negative emotions, we can decide how we will view it.

When we associate into a situation, we imagine ourselves as a player and feel that we are being personally affected by what is happening. If, for instance, we are feeling distant from God, we can imagine ourselves in his presence, and that imagination will cause emotions to change.

On the other side, if we are experiencing negative emotions that cause us to not want to be in the presence of God, we can imagine that we are outside observers of the situation. We can actually watch (imagine) ourselves interacting with the negative thing as if we were watching someone else. As a disassociated bystander our emotions tone down.

Intentional Thinking

Typically we don't sit down and decide that we are going to feel bad. Bad feelings are electrical and chemical events that happen in our bodies that we interpret to be bad. Bad feelings were designed by God to be a helpful thing for us. They warn us when there is some kind of problem that we need to deal with.

But sometimes we create emotional habits which cause us to get into a state of feeling bad when we shouldn't. Instead of dealing with a negative event, we sometime just sit on it. This allows the bad feelings to become ingrained to the point that we get a negative response, even at times when it is not appropriate.

As human beings, we have the ability to think our way out of it. When we feel a certain feeling, we automatically interpret that feeling to mean something. If we learn to recognize the feeling, we can actually interpret it a different way.

For instance, if you were talking with someone and they said something to you that seemed insulting, you don't have to interpret it as an insult. In your mind you could turn it around and realize that the other person said it out of ignorance. That way you make the problem theirs, rather than taking it on yourself. Taking it on yourself causes you to associate into negative feelings. Putting it back on them allows you to disassociate from them. I am not saying that this is an easy process. Depending on the strength of the feelings, it can be quite hard. But we are created in such a way that we can be the master of our body rather than its slave.

Eye Placement

Another very interesting way of taking control of emotion relates to eye placement. If you are not familiar with this concept, it may seem rather strange, but it is a very powerful tool. In a general sense, various activities in your body have been assigned to different areas your brain. When you access those activities, your eyes automatically react in a particular way.

For instance, imagine the house you lived in when you were a child. Stop! Before you read on, go ahead and imagine the house - the size, shape, what the front looked like, etc. If you are like most people, your eyes shot up and to the left when you stopped to remember it. In fact, you may have actually even turned your whole head that way.

Now then, pretend that you need to go shopping for some groceries and you need to get three items. What three items will you get? Don't continue reading until you have made your shopping list of three items. Now, if you are like most people, when you began to consider the items your eyes shot up and to the right.

Now, what is happening? Our brains have assigned visual memory and creative activity to the positions we have just experienced. Up and to the left relates to memories. Up and to the right relates to creating or constructing things.

The same process also works with our auditory processes. The left side of our head (around the ear) relates to auditory memory and the right side of our head (again around the ear) relates to our auditory creative functions.

So far you may find this interesting but are wondering what this has to do with emotions. Well, there is another aspect of this that relates to feelings, and this is where we want to go with this. Most people access their feelings down and to the right. You can actually remember, feel or generate emotion by locating your eyes this way. For instance, if you want to "feel" the presence of God, use your imagination and picture him being next to you. When you have the picture, take your eyes down to your midsection.

Remember, this does not relate to where God actually is, only to how you experience him emotionally. Having a feeling that God is really next to you might be a big help in your prayer experience. It may help you concentrate better and keep you more motivated to spend time with him.

Do Something

This knowledge is meaningless unless you actually put it into practice. The purpose of this discussion is to give you more of an edge as you engage God in conversation. Over time you can train your emotions so that you don't have to consciously use these mechanisms, but in the "getting started" phase you may find them very useful.

Physical Control Part II - The Stamina

Have you ever been going through a typical day and all of a sudden you realized that you were just completely out of energy? Perhaps it was a drop in your blood sugar or you were just physically exhausted, but it was like you hit a wall - it was hard to mentally focus, you felt muscle fatigue, maybe even sleepy. You may have even gotten a headache and began acting grumpy at those around you. Even though you might be one of the most competent people in the world in your field, at that moment your ability to function effectively simply went out the window.

A deep and ongoing interaction with God is not, typically, something that is easy. When we actively engage the spiritual arena, we enter a war zone. Certainly God wants us to be engaged with him, but there are evil spiritual beings who are doing all they can to keep us separated from him. When we seriously take on the commitment to personally engage God, we have to recognize that it requires a lot of physical energy.

It takes energy to gain and maintain control of our emotions. It takes energy to discipline our bodies for spiritual interaction. It takes energy to concentrate and maintain the focus of our minds on spiritual activity. When we don't work to keep our bodies fit for these activities, we will find it more difficult to engage effectively in prayer.

We will not spend a lot of time getting into the specifics of physical fitness. It is helpful, however, to at least mention the areas that we must pay attention to, if we are to strengthen our bodies for spiritual engagement.

Nutrition

Nutrition relates to the kinds of nutrients that we put into our bodies. It takes a lot of physical energy to become good in prayer, and these nutrients are the source of our energy.

We need to be sure that the foods we eat support our health. We need to be sure we are providing ourselves with all of the nutrients that our cells need to stay healthy and productive.

Nutrition also relates to how much we eat. We need to be sure that we don't overeat, which causes our bodies to store fat and accumulate wastes. We also have to be sure that we don't undereat and deprive the body of the nutrients it needs to function effectively.

Rest

A second aspect of physical health relates to rest. Our bodies are built in such a way that they require a certain amount of rest in order to stay healthy. This is not something that we normally think a lot about as we plan our health regimen, but it must not be left out if we want to achieve peak performance.

There is a reason that many cults deliberately deprive new initiates of sleep. There is a reason one of the first things torturers do to those they want to break is to deprive them of sleep. Lack of sleep breaks a person down emotionally, physically and mentally.

To develop and maintain physical stamina, it is necessary to get enough rest. One of the most common themes that you hear when people share their prayer struggles is that they fall asleep while praying. Proper rest can help solve stamina problems.

Exercise

It might seem odd, to some, that physical exercise is something that will contribute to more effective praying. However, it is absolutely true. The better your physical conditioning the better able you will be to engage God. There are several factors that come into play here.

First, a stronger body means more stamina. As a result, when fighting the enemy you will be able to stay in the fight longer.

A second factor is that exercise eliminates toxins from the body. Toxins in the body are a primary cause of illness and disease. Our lymph system - the waste removal system - does not have a pump. Muscle movement is necessary to move the wastes, that our cells produce, into the blood stream and out of the body.

Finally, physical exercise, particularly aerobic exercise, puts more oxygen into our systems. Oxygen is our primary source of energy.

Get with the Program

Let's not get this concept out of its proper perspective. If you are capable of developing your body to that of a world class athlete, then of course that is going to be of great benefit to you. But that is not where we are going with this. Not everyone can achieve the same level of fitness for one reason or another. Age, injury or illness may limit what you can do. But everyone who is conscious can do something. All we are saying, here, is that the stronger you can keep your body, the easier it will be to master the parts of it that become physical hindrances to praying.

Most people don't consider getting physically fit and maintaining that fitness as a spiritual exercise. While a fitness program may not be spiritual in and of itself, it can be a great benefit as we attempt to operate in the spiritual arena.

We are spiritual beings, but we are housed in a physical body. Whether we like it or not, the limitations that are imposed on us because of that are daunting. Physical conditioning does not just happen. We have to make a concerted effort to make it a priority. To the degree we pick up the challenge, we will be in a position to be more effective in our interaction with God.

Physical Control Part III -The Brain

A few years ago I was in Sweden and visited a science museum. It was a very interesting, and quite "hands on," program designed with children in mind. Each section of the museum dealt with different fields of science. In the biology section was a display on the brain that I found quite fascinating.

In this display there was a helmet that had electrodes in it. Wires, then, ran from the electrodes into a computer. On the computer screen was a dot. It took me a couple of minutes to get the hang of this apparatus, but when I put the helmet on I was able to manipulate the movement of the dot on the computer screen just by thinking about it. My brain waves did the work.

Now, I don't have a clue how I made that dot move but, since I did it myself, I know that it was not a hoax. The operation of my brain is not magic. There are actual chemical and electrical actions going on that can be measured, captured, processed and manipulated.

Our mind and our brains are not the same thing. Our minds operate as a function of our spirit. The brain is that part of our physical being that processes and stores sensory information from our environment, and runs the automatic processes of our bodies. That being said, there is a dynamic and essential interplay between the two parts.

Since the brain is a physical organ, it is subject to the physical dynamics of the body. It can become lazy and sluggish, undisciplined, and unfocused. On the other hand, we are able to develop our brains so that they are more effective in supporting the various activities we do. This includes our ability to interact in the spiritual arena with God. There are several areas where we can develop our brain power which, in turn, support our ability to pray.

Content

In order to function in life, it is necessary to have a certain amount of information to work with. We obtain this information in the process of living life. Some of it we get from specific study, some we get from experience, some we just pick up along the way.

We gain much of this information whether we are trying to or not. We are wired to be able to do it. But, it is possible to get better at it than we already are. By practicing, we can become better at storing information which strengthens our ability to do Bible study and various ministry activities.

Brain Flexibility

Brain flexibility relates to how quickly we process information. Things we are more familiar with we process more quickly, and vice versa. It is possible to gain quickness by working with materials, or with situations, over and over until we become proficient.

This can be helpful when we find ourselves in situations where we are called on to share information about spiritual matters with people who need that kind of encouragement. Having this kind of quickness can also be of great benefit in our interaction with God, particularly in the area of discerning and responding to his communications to us.

Outlook

Outlook involves our ability to shift back and forth between an objective and subjective viewpoint. There are times when we need to be able to see things as a dispassionate observer, and other times when we need to be able to mentally put ourselves into a situation. This has already been dealt with above in the section on emotions. It is possible to work on this skill until we are able to shift back and forth at will.

The ability to produce this shift makes it easier to enter the mental state that is most helpful, at any given moment, to promote a relationship with God. It is easier to feel the presence of God when we enter into the subjective mode, and it is easier to deal with personal struggles when we can become more objective.

Concentration

Concentration relates to the length of time a person is able to stay focused on a particular matter. This is another brain function that can be developed with the proper effort.

The value of this skill should be obvious when it comes to praying. One of the most difficult things for most people to do while praying is to stay focused. The better your concentration the more effective your time with God.

Focus

Focus has to do with the scope of a person's mental activity. It is possible to focus very tightly on a small detail, to zoom out and see the big picture, or go any place in between. It is possible to develop the ability to do this beyond what naturally comes to us in the course of life.

As we relate to God about different matters, we need to be able to find the appropriate focus point for each of the things we are discussing with him. Interceding for another person calls on us to focus tightly. Praying for our country calls for a wider focus.

The better we are able to do this, the more effective will be our communication with God.

Paradigm Control

Paradigm control involves our ability to switch from one perspective to another. For instance, we can mentally view an image in our mind from the top, the right side, from the inside or a host of other angles. We can consider a decision we need to make by running through many possibilities before we make the decision. We can see something from our own viewpoint or from another person's perspective. This ability to shift paradigms is useful because it gives us the ability to mentally work through situations before we actually have to deal with them in real life. It can also be developed if we put the effort into it.

Paradigm control is also helpful as we interact with God. For one thing, we need to be able to see things from God's perspective when making life decisions. Then, when trying to discern his direction for our lives, we need to be able to consider the possibilities, as well as the consequences, of various actions.

Have At It

Developing our brain activity can have a powerful effect on our ability to effectively interact with God. By becoming more skilled in using our brains we become able to engage God more effectively and to understand his way of thinking and living life.

This brain development occurs naturally to a certain extent but, after a point, everyone will hit their limit. This limit, however, is not absolute. It is possible to take each of the brain functions above and push them to higher levels. To do that, though, requires a deliberate and concerted effort. Do it and you will find your ability to communicate with God going to ever higher levels.

A Means Not an End

When it comes to spiritual development, none of the things mentioned in this chapter are an end in themselves. It is certainly possible to think that they are. It is also possible to work on developing our emotional capacity, our physical endurance and our mental agility just for the sake of improving our lives. And developing those abilities are not bad goals to have for life development.

However, when considering the way this all relates to your interaction with God, you need to have a different understanding. These aspects of your being are actually tools which can help you in your praying. As you strengthen the emotional elements of life, you become more able to work through the physical and spiritual struggles that you inevitably face. As you strengthen your body, you develop the stamina to engage the spiritual opposition that you face. And, as you strengthen your brain activity, you become more effective in relating to, and understanding, God and his ways.

But make no mistake about it. All of this requires effort. You cannot just live life according to your old routines and expect to grow in your ability to use your physical body to engage the spiritual realm. It is not the wimp who is going to be able to experience this higher level of interaction with God. It is only for the person who is willing to put forth the effort to move to a higher level.

Digging Deeper

- In the past, have you ever given any thought about the interaction of your physical and spiritual parts? Do you believe that you are capable of developing to a higher level spiritually by strengthening your physical parts?

- Think about the times when you pray. What are the biggest physical obstacles you struggle with during that time? What do you think you should do to get beyond those obstacles?

- Make a list of each of the areas of physical development listed in this chapter. Under each category, make a plan to strengthen that part of your life as a part of your spiritual development process.

I have experienced the act of praying in two different ways. I believe that the first one is more common, but it is the second one that takes us to the ultimate destination of personal interaction with God.

The first is mechanical. This is the process of working through a formula to take us from the beginning to the end of our communication to God. In the process of learning how to operate in the spiritual realm I depended on this method because my growth had not taken me to the place where I could go further. But when I came to the place where I was able to make the shift to an actual personal interaction with God, I left this completely behind.

My ultimate goal in praying has always been to interact with God. This is not mechanical, but spiritual and personal. There is nothing more profound in my life than my interaction with God.

In the period of my life when praying tended to be more mechanical, I had to struggle to maintain the willpower to go before God consistently. With a focus on personal interaction, that is never an issue. In the mechanical mode I was always trying to figure out what to say to him. Now, we converse back and forth about any and everything at any time.

I wish I was further along than I am, but I continue to grow. I, also, wish I could simply hand off to you the ability to interact with God personally and intimately, but that is your journey. I promise, it will be worth it to you to take it on.

Chapter 7
Developing the Discipline to Pray

The day I tested for my third degree black belt in karate was one of the hardest days I can ever remember. It was basically an endurance test. I endured nearly twelve hours of agonizing exertion that pushed me to the very limit of my being. The first barrier I came up against was physical. After several hours of vigorous exertion I was taken to the point of near total exhaustion. On top of that, my feet were killing me. The tenderness and fatigue were almost beyond my ability to bear.

Then I came up against the second barrier, which proved to be even more difficult than the first - my spiritual boundaries. As I continued, hour after hour, and the pain and fatigue grew, I found myself consciously coming to a decision point. I had to decide if I was going to keep going on in spite of the pain, or if I would quit. I honestly felt like quitting. In fact, there were several times that I wondered to myself, "What stupidity is driving a 50-year-old man to go through this?" My body was screaming at me to give up - and the longer I continued the louder it screamed.

At first, the question of whether or not to continue only crossed my mind occasionally. But after a point, I was having to make a deliberate decision to keep going with virtually every movement I made. But, I did it! I disciplined my body and my spirit, and persevered to the end. As a result I was able to achieve my goal and advance in my martial arts training.

As I was going through the process I questioned the value of it. But now, having the perspective of hindsight, I deeply value the qualities it has brought out in my life.

It is one thing to understand all we need to know in order to pray effectively. We can understand what prayer is, who God is, who we are, all the elements of prayer, how to engage God and all the rest. But intellectual understanding is not praying. For all of this to have any meaning whatsoever, we must actually get down to the process of praying - and this is where the going gets tough. This is where wimps quit.

We have already alluded to much of the difficulty. We struggle emotionally, as we wrestle with quieting our minds or with our own feelings of unworthiness to enter into the presence of God. We struggle physically, as we attempt to ramp up the energy to engage God. We struggle mentally, to concentrate and stay focused.

But as important as these things are in our efforts to make our praying more effective, they are not the deciding issues. Those are merely processes and operations that help us wade through the physical limitations that we struggle against. The real key to more effective praying lies in spiritual development, not in physical processes.

What, exactly, does that mean? Well, consider this. We don't act out our lives based on our surface desires or on our "oughts." There are a lot of things we "want" in life but which we don't consider a high enough priority to make them a reality - and we could go after them if we had the motivation. There are a lot of things in life that we know we "ought" to do, but just don't. Why is that? Why is it that we don't pursue the things we say we want, and the things we know we ought to do?

Some will point to the issues we spoke of in the previous chapter and say that we have simply developed habits that take us in other directions. Others will claim that we just haven't ramped up the emotional intensity enough to make necessary changes. There is a certain amount of truth to these observations but, again, these are side issues. Physical processes can help us move forward to a degree, but the motivation to take that new direction has to come from someplace else - from our spirit.

What we have to do is somehow get beyond the surface issues and go all the way down to our very core desires. It is our core desires that we act out in daily life - and these sometimes actually work against our surface desires and wants.

Let's use praying as an example. Chances are, since you are reading this book, you have a desire to be more effective in your praying. What that means is, you have a sense that you ought to be more effective, and you have a surface desire to do it. But there is something that keeps you from actually carrying it out. What is that "something?"

As hard as it may be to swallow, you will have to face up to a profound truth if you ever want to get beyond your current struggles. If you struggle with being consistent and persistent in prayer, it is because your core desire does not include spending time with God. There are other desires that you have which are stronger. Your core desires will **always** be what you act out in life.

So what are they? Well, they are different for each person, but to get a hint about yours, consider what you do - that's right, what you do. If you have a choice to pray or watch TV, which do you do? If you have a choice to spend time with God or sleep a little later, which do you do? If you have a choice to pray or go to a movie or a ball game, which do you do? This is not to say that we should not do those other things, but what are you are willing to put aside in order to spend time with God? When you can honestly answer that last question, you will have discovered where praying fits in your personal system of core desires.

Developing the discipline for praying is certainly within the realm of possibility. Let's look at four keys to developing that discipline.

- Lay Your Motivational Foundation
- Take the Right Actions
- Ramp Up Your Intensity
- Pray Relationally

Lay Your Motivational Foundation

There are, actually, a number of different ways to increase your motivation for praying, but there are three underlying issues that you must embrace. If you can do these, your motivation to spend time with God will ramp up to the highest level possible. The three things relate to 1) what you believe, 2) what you love and 3) what you decide.

Shore Up Your Belief

The beliefs that we are talking about here are the ones that animate your action. Ask most people, who claim to be Christians, if they believe in God, and they will certainly tell you, "Yes!" But the real question should be, "Who is the God you believe in?" A person whose God is impersonal may not even see a need to pray. And even if they do, it is out of a sense of fear or obligation. A person whose God is subjective will not even consider personal interaction with him to be possible. A person who sees God as a cosmic "Santa Clause" will beg for stuff but not give himself to God in return. And there are people who claim to be Christians who fit into all three of these categories.

There are a lot of ways to conceive of God, and each one will take you to a different form of interaction with him. It is essential, then, to understand who God really is, and to interact with him according to that reality. God is personal and has created mankind in a way that makes it possible for us to have an intimate relationship with him. Anyone who doesn't believe in that kind of God will not try to interact with him personally.

Now, here is the problem. Many people who say that they believe in a personal God, don't live their lives as if he were personal. So what does that mean? It means that even though they acknowledge a personal God intellectually, their core belief is different. Anyone who believes that God is personal, the way the Bible describes him, will engage him in a personal and intimate relationship.

So, here is the test. Look at your interaction with God. Look at your praying. What is it like? Is it all one way conversation? Is it all asking for stuff? Is it directed to some impersonal "something" out there? If you do not conceive of God as a real person with whom you have a powerful loving relationship, there is a serious problem with your belief system. Your first order of business must be to dig into God's revelation and come to an understanding of who he really is.

Strengthen Your Love

Once your belief system is in order, the next thing you must do is fall in love. It is certainly possible to know someone but not really like them. But if you desire deep intimacy, you will have to develop a deep love between yourself and the other person, and real praying assumes this kind of relationship exists between you and God.

Let's try to reduce this down to the lowest common denominator. The deepest motivation that causes us to do whatever it is that we do is love. Put another way, we do what we love. If we find that we would rather do some particular activity more than we want to spend time with God, we love that thing more.

If you really do love God, you will find time to spend with him. It is as simple as that. So here is the test. Do you spend intimate time with God, or not? Do you crave that intimate interaction with him? Do you actively look for opportunities to spend more time with him? Your answers to these questions will be very telling. It doesn't matter how much you say you love God, if you are not intimate with him your love is lacking.

Make the Right Decisions

The last factor that will get you where you need to be in your relationship with God relates to the decisions you make. Relationship with God may result in having certain feelings, but the relationship itself is not a feeling. Ultimately your relationship with God rests on what you decide the relationship will be.

If you struggle with bad praying because of a problem with belief, then you can decide that you will do your due diligence and come to a proper understanding of who God really is. Once you decide that is what you are going to do, you will be able to go through a process that leads you to the truth that will solve the belief issue.

If you struggle with bad praying because of a problem with loving "things" more than you love God, then you can decide that you will do what is necessary to get the relationship where it needs to be.

Whether it is a matter of confessing sin, putting aside some idol in your life or simply giving your life to him fully, you can change the direction of your life by a decision. Once you firmly decide that God will be your first love, you will be on the road to a personal relationship with him like you have never known before.

Take the Right Actions

Taking the right actions for praying means to get the conversation going. Don't just study talking, actually do it! There are two directions that a conversation must move - away from you and toward you.

Talk

The "away from" part is where you talk. This should not be too difficult because it is probably where you have put most of the emphasis in your praying up until now. Give God praise and thanksgiving. Confess your offenses and turn away from them. Ask him for things that help you and other people. Talk about the decisions you need to make. Talk about the weather. Talk to him about everything that goes on in your life. Talk and talk and talk, then talk some more. You can never engage God too much in conversation.

Bible Study

But don't let all of the conversation be talking. Engage yourself in the "toward you" part, too. You have to take some time to listen, as well. For most people this will be the hardest part because they have never taken the time to get good at it. So take the time, starting now. Here's how you do it.

To study the Bible does not mean to just open it up and read. The Bible is not just a book. It is, literally, the revelation of God. In it he has revealed himself and his ways. When you dig into it you have to read it as if God is teaching you directly - which he is. So, when you read a story, there is a lesson in it for you. When you read a command, it is a command for you. When you gain a new insight, that is an insight for you to apply to your life. It is personal. It is God's way of speaking to you. Take it as such.

Meditation

Meditation is a very powerful communication tool that God wants to use in your life, but very few people actually open this channel. Meditation is not where you clear your mind and try to let God pump something into it. In fact, it is quite the opposite. Meditation is active. When we meditate, we meditate "on" something. The most effective thing to meditate on is a portion of the revelation.

Start by memorizing a short passage of scripture. This is important because you are then free to focus on the message. Then, in your mind, begin to go over and over the passage, one word at a time, and think about the meaning. You will find yourself gaining new insights that you never even considered before, as God begins to share with you the depth of the meaning of his revelation.

Engage the Holy Spirit

Of course it is God, speaking to us Spirit-to-spirit, that gives us his side of the communication process as we read the Bible and meditate. But God is not limited in his speaking to those ways. He can speak directly to our spirit if we learn how to listen to him.

We must be careful with this, however. There have been many people, over the years, who have claimed to have a word from God and it was just plain false. God will never tell us something that goes against what he has revealed to us in his revelation. If a person claims that God has spoken and it results in thinking, speaking or acting in ways contrary to what God has revealed to us in the Bible, it is a false claim.

God does not reveal to us new beliefs or values. What he does reveal is personal information related to how we are to apply his revelation to our lives individually. God let me know that I was supposed to become a missionary and that he wanted me to become a pastor. He has a calling for every believer and he will communicate that directly to those who open themselves to hear it.

Explaining how to receive this communication is a struggle, though. It happens in our hearts. It requires that we have established a relationship with God by receiving Jesus Christ into our lives, and that we conform our lives to God's values and standards of behavior. Once we have put ourselves into a position to communicate with him, we have to spend time with him learning how to listen and discern his communications to us. The process can't be explained in words since it happens completely on a spiritual level, but it does happen when we position ourselves for it.

Ramp Up Your Intensity

Intensity can be expressed in very different ways. The way it is expressed can make a huge difference in the outcome - especially as it relates to relationships.

It can be expressed as uncontrolled passion. There certainly is powerful emotion in the person who expresses intensity this way, but there is also a huge lack of discipline. It is like the wild stallion running free on the range. It is beautiful, powerful and able to express itself freely, but it is not much use for anything but to look at.

Intensity can also be expressed as controlled passion. This is like the martial artist who looks completely and perfectly calm with every movement under complete control. And while on the surface everything seems calm and collected, when he strikes out at his target, boards break and tiles shatter. Why is the competent martial artist so cool and calm under stress? Because he has trained and trained to the point that, no matter what happens, he knows exactly what to do. There is no need for an outburst.

For many people, praying is a desperate attempt to get God to pay attention and give them the desires of their hearts. The person praying this way is like the wild stallion. Praying becomes a wrestling match or a desperate struggle - full of intensity but totally out of control. They beg and plead with God to give them what they want - whether it is a material object or to grant healing or keep their loved one alive.

But we don't need to feel this kind of struggle when we are fully confident in God and his operation and direction in our lives. God has his plan and it is perfect. God has everything under absolute control, whether we understand what that means or not. If we have developed our spirit to the point where we are able to have that kind of confidence in him, we will never be panicked when things seemingly go wrong. In the face of what appears to be the worst of all situations, we can be like the martial artist who stands calm and composed before his opponent. We have to understand that life is not about "me," it is about God. If "I" begin feeling desperation, I have made it all about "me."

Once you have your life pointed in the right direction, as it relates to belief and love, and have made the decision that you are going to focus your life in a relationship with God, the only thing left is to live it out. This is where the feelings, the stamina and the brains come into play. Once you are moving in the right direction, you have the ability to intensify what you are doing.

This intensification is basically the manipulation of your physical parts - emotions, body and brains. To do this you simply exert more energy into the relationship with God. You take the principles related to developing the physical parts of your being and apply them to your praying.

You don't necessarily have to jump up and down and scream, but you can ramp up your emotions by becoming enthusiastic about your relationship with God. By expending physical energy you can make your body feel better. By putting more energy into your brain activity (focus, concentration, etc.), you can make yourself more able to get after your praying.

These things are not the praying, itself. But once you have the beliefs, love and decisions under control, these support activities will help you to be more effective in maintaining your excitement about being with God. And if you have trained yourself well, your intensity will be controlled and powerful as you recognize that God always has things in hand.

Pray Relationally

I love watching football. I especially love watching my college alma mater play - at least when they are winning. As I watch a game, I definitely get emotionally involved. When the good guys are winning, I feel good. When something bad happens, I feel bad. But no matter which way it is going, I assure you that I am putting my whole energy into my cheering. If you were next to me watching the game, you would have no doubt about my loyalties.

Haven't you experienced the same thing in your life? Don't you, or haven't you, had a team or a person that you felt so connected to that you poured your whole being into supporting them? Why can't we make our relationship with God like that? Wow! What would it be like if we got as pumped up about seeing God win in the world as we do about seeing our football team win on the field?

I have lived most of my life as a Christian. I have tried to focus my life in a way that would bring me closer and closer to God. I have always recognized that praying is an essential part of the process. But praying is not for wimps. It requires a lot of discipline. It requires a lot of understanding. It requires a lot of training. It requires a lot of time with attention directed to God. It requires putting a huge amount of energy into the relationship.

Getting into a relationship with God is easy. Just ask him into your life. But if you think that living in that relationship is easy, you have deceived yourself. It is a struggle. It is a war.

But while there is struggle, it is not agony. The deepest satisfactions I have ever experienced in life have been those times when I have gone after things that were good, right, and extremely difficult, and was able to see them through to the end. Success is sweet! And the sweetest success I have ever had in my life is my relationship with God!

There are different levels of relationship, and the way you pray is a reflection of your relationship with God. Do you give yourself wholly to him? Half way? Just a little bit?

One of the important and powerful metaphors that describes the relationship that believers have with Christ is that of a bride. In Ephesians 5:22-32, Paul goes to great lengths to make a close comparison between the relationship of a husband and wife to that of Christ and his church. While we can read this in a way that depersonalizes the meaning to be Christ and his relationship to the *institution* of church, that is not the way a relationship works. It is the most intimate and personal of all interactions. While it is true that the metaphor of the bride refers to the collective body of believers, the way that the interaction works in our physical reality is between Christ and individual believers, who are members of the body. In other words we have to think of ourselves, individually, as the bride of Christ.

So, is your relationship with him intimate like a spouse, or is it somewhat impersonal, as an acquaintance? If it is impersonal, you won't give yourself to it 100%. If it is intimate and personal, there will be nothing more important in your life - and your actions will prove it!

I must say that, in spite of my many years of trying to understand this prayer thing, it has only been in recent times that I have come to understand it in a way that allows me to feel satisfied in my praying. Not that I have reached perfection, but I am now able to get deep with God in a way that I have never been able to do before. What you have read in this book are my insights. I had to come to the place, personally, where I understood that praying, at its core, is not a mental activity as much as it is a spiritual one - a relationship. I also had to figure out that praying, at its core, is experiential; and I am still striving to better understand the experience.

The purpose of praying is not to make yourself feel good. Feeling good is not a bad thing, and I actually recommend that you do it as often as possible. But praying aims for a different outcome. Its purpose is to allow you to live your life in an active relationship with the creator of the universe - the one who created all of material reality for a purpose (his purpose), and is working to bring about a specific outcome. It allows you to get in on what he is doing, not just to know what it is. And it allows you to work side by side with God to accomplish that purpose. How powerful is it that we can actually have a meaningful part in fulfilling the cosmic purposes of God? The "feel good" part is simply a bonus.

As you contemplate your praying, you must realize that everything that is written in this book is simply a starting point. I promise you, if you master everything in the book your relationship with God will take on a depth that you could never before have imagined. That being said, mastery of the processes are only the beginning of the journey. If you get it all, you will only be a beginner. A relationship with God provides for a level of depth that far outpaces anything you can now imagine, no matter where you are spiritually.

God is a real person and he created us special so that he would have like beings to relate to personally. We have a choice as to how we will allow this to play out in our lives. Now the choice is personal to you. Don't allow yourself to wimp out now. Take it on! Make it real! Get intimate with God!

Digging Deeper

- Think about when you pray. How personal do you get with God? How intense is your interaction with God?

- What would you have to do to take the knowledge of how to pray, and apply it in your life in a way that makes it routine and powerful?

- Close your eyes right now and step into the presence of God. Offer your life to him. Let him touch you. Embrace him. Talk and listen to him. Enjoy his presence with you.

Notes

Chapter 3
[1] Gen 1:1
[2] 1 John 4:19
[3] John 1:12
[4] Daniel 4:35
[5] Isa 53:6
[6] John 3:14-15
[7] Col 1:22-23
[8] John 3:16
[9] John 3:18

Chapter 4
[1] Lam 3:25, Dan 2:20, Eph 3:20, Heb 13:15
[2] 1 Chron 16:34, Ps 4:7, Ps 106:47, Matt 15:36, Luke 2:38
[3] Gen 18:22-33, Ex 32:11-14, 1 Sam 12:23, Luke 22:31-32, Acts 12:5-17
[4] Gen 4:13-16, Num 16:15, Ps 102:1-2, Matt 6:9-10, 2 Cor 12:7-10
[5] Ex 32:31-34, Num 5:5-7, 1 Sam 12:10-11, James 5:16-18, 1 John 1:9
[6] Judg 10:16-18, Ps 38, Lam 1:20-22
[7] Job 30-31, Jer 12:1-4
[8] Gen 15:1-6, Ex 3:7-22, Job 7, Ps 85
[9] 1 Sam 1:10-16, Ps 51:10-13, Ps 86
[10] Job 1:20-22, Ps 31:1-5, Matt 26:39-44, Eph 5:19-20
[11] Gen 24:63, Deut 9:18-21, 1 Sam 1:10-16, Matt 18:19-20, John 4:22-24, Acts 16:25
[12] Ps 31, Isa 1:18, Jer 15:15-16:1, John 17, Heb 4:15-16

[13] Job 21:13-15, Dan 9:3-19, Matt 23:14, Luke 20:46-47
[14] 1 Kings 18:36-38, 2 Kings 6:17-20, 1 Chron 4:10, Matt 7:7-11, Acts 12:5-17
[15] Acts 9:10-19
[16] Jer 17:14-27, Jer 32:24-25, Amos 5:4-6, Luke 21:36, Luke 22:39-46
[17] Ezek 20:31, Hos 5:5-7, Mic 3:4, Mark 12:38-40

Chapter 5
[1] John 4:16
[2] Psalm 99:9
[3] Daniel 9:9
[4] James 1:5
[5] Luke 18:19
[6] Psalm 97:1-2
[7] 2 Peter 3:9
[8] Luke 22:39-46

Dr. Freddy Davis is involved in a wide variety of ministry activities. His is currently an, author, seminar speaker, pastor and the owner of TSM Enterprises.

In addition to the "*Wimp*" books, he is the author of the book ***Supercharged!***, as well as the audio album ***Supercharge Yourself!*** He has also authored the "*Nutshell*" series of books.

Freddy received his BS in Communications from Florida State University as well as an MDiv and DMin from Southwestern Baptist Theological Seminary. He spent 16½ years overseas serving as a missionary (11½ years in Japan and 5 years in the former Soviet Republic of Latvia).

As a conference speaker, Freddy speaks to businesses and other organizations on the topics of personal development, decision making, influence, and leadership. All of his writing and speaking is based on the premise that "being" precedes "doing." A person must *become* the kind of person who is successful in order to see success happen in life.

Freddy is also available to churches and Christian organizations to speak on the topics of praying, understanding the culture war and how worldview affects your ability to faithfully live the Christian life.

For more information...
On speaking engagements or other
resources from Dr. Freddy Davis,
Contact him by e-mail: davis@iname.com
Or fax him at 850-514-4571.
Also, visit his website at http://www.tsmenterprises.com

Made in the USA
Charleston, SC
28 September 2010